# A TALE OF TWO VILLAGES

## MARLOES IN THE 1930s
## DALE IN THE 1940s

Merrivale

Cover photographs  The Marloes Clock and the Brig quay Dale

Published by Lloyd Jones
246 Christchurch Road, Newport, NP19 8BJ

Printed by  A Print Newport
ISBN      978-0-9536982-6-4

# ACKNOWLEDGMENTS

I am most grateful to Ann, the wife of the late Peter James and their son, Paul who were ever ready to refresh, verify and in one or two instances, correct my memory of many happy times at Marloes Court and the village. Michael James, Peter's brother was also a great help in this context. Marjorie Johnson was a rich and authoritative source of reminiscence and detail on all matters concerning the area and very ready to share and authenticate my happy memories of Dale and I am most grateful to her too. I would also like to thank Mil Reynolds of Dale who has been a great help in distributing this book.

My cousins, Peter Davies and George Harries of Merrivale Publishers have been encouraging and supportive throughout and I can say with total confidence that if it had not been for them, A Tale of Two Villages would never have seen the light of day. They, if not the actual parents of this little book, are entirely responsible for its conception and latterly saw it through a difficult labour and ultimate delivery. Judy, my wife and Sarah, my daughter have also been great supports and made helpful suggestions.

My thanks also to Ted Goddard for sharing his knowledge of the maritime history of the area and for Vernon Scott who put me right on other matters.

Haverfordwest Record Office offered willing assistance in making available records and maps.

My thanks also to Roger of A Print, Newport who has been a great help.

# INTRODUCTION

Pembrokeshire is a singular county yet for most of our countrymen it remains comparatively unknown and unappreciated even in these days of easy motor way communications. Perhaps we should be thankful that because of its remoteness it is still not a major tourist destination. It is favoured by a discerning minority who value its peace and quiet, the space it offers and the time it spares for its visitors. If Pembrokeshire is relatively remote, the villages of Marloes and Dale, the hamlet of St Brides and the peninsula which forms the Southern arm of St Bride's Bay and where I grew up, must surely count as some of its remoter parts. Marloes is about 55 miles from Junction 49 at the end of the M4 and from here a 5 hour drive to the Chiswick Flyover.

The Marloes and Dale that I am going to describe is 264 miles from London and, including stops for petrol, relief and refreshment, (the three events not always coinciding in the 1930s) this journey meant at least 12 hours' hard driving on the A40 from Haverfordwest. The route lay through the town centres of Carmarthen, Brecon, Abergavenny, Monmouth, Ross, Gloucester and Cheltenham. Then came the temporary relief of the Oxford bypass before passing through High Wycombe, Beaconsfield and Gerrard's Cross eventually reaching the London suburbs. Although pre war traffic was barely a trickle, the motor car of the 1930s and the roads that it used made it impossible to sustain an average of much above 25 m.p.h. Few people ever ventured as far as London and it's hardly surprising that if anyone did travel that far, they went by rail. The fastest train in 1938 was the 11.47 a.m. from Haverfordwest which took 6 hours 25 minutes and arrived at Paddington usually dead on time at 6.10 p.m.

The 1930s and 40s are also becoming relatively remote and whilst this is in no sense a historical piece, I hope I will be able to convey some of the flavour of life in Marloes from 1935 to1941 and in Dale from 1942 to 1948. I have tried wherever possible to describe things in chronological order but it has been necessary here and there in order to provide some continuity, to retrace our steps. It is an attempt to provide insights into a very special part of the country in times of peace, the economic depression that reigned throughout much of the U.K. and the war that followed.

I was born in May 1930 in Puncheston, a village more than 400 feet above sea level in the Preseli Hills of Pembrokeshire. My father, Trefor Lloyd Jones was headmaster of the Primary School in this scattered and remote community.The school register contained about 30 names. It was his first "headship" after having taught earlier in places as diverse as Croydon and Llanrhian. It was at Llanrhian, a small village between St David's and Fishguard, that he met my mother Lilian Sime, a native of St David's. Her sister, Muriel, was married to the headmaster of Llanrhian, Bryn Davies.They will reappear in due course.

It was at this time that my father developed symptoms of peptic ulceration which troubled him for a large part of the rest of his life. Led to believe that part of the trouble was due to the drinking water, our stay in Puncheston was fairly brief. In 1933 we moved to Madeley in Shropshire where my father taught as an assistant teacher in the Church School.

We lived in a flat in a fairly large house, "The Furlongs", formerly the home of onetime celebrity Captain Webb, the first man to swim the English Channel. The move to Shropshire was at least partly due to the fact that my mother's brother, John Sime was the vicar of Madeley.

I had been baptised John Owen and now we were living just a few doors away from the Vicarage where Uncle John and his son "Young John" lived. With this trio of Johns I can't explain why I wasn't then called Owen but ever since, except during National Service and afterwards in the T.A., I was generally known in polite circles at least, as Lloyd. This has resulted in me being introduced on more than one occasion as "Lloyd Lloyd Jones" and at other times to the suggestion that not wishing to be just plain "Jones", I had acquired a double barrel name.

It was in Madeley that I have my first clear memory. Just as well, you may say, because this was the occasion of my first marriage. I was 4 and had just married my cousin Mary aged 6. She was Uncle John's only daughter. Following tradition, the reception was held in the bride's home which had a large sloping garden with a perimeter path enclosing a central lawn. It was literally a runaway marriage because, driving away to our honeymoon in our imaginary car, a Wolseley Hornet, we raced down the path. Mary's white head dress streamed out behind her as we ran. Like Mr Toad of Wind in the Willows, I was smoking a cigar in the form of a wooden twig which I held between clenched teeth. As I steered one handed down the path, Mary clutching my left arm, I tripped and the cigar cut my palate causing great distress and the end of the honeymoon.

Unfortunately the change of water did nothing for my father's ulcer problem and in 1935 we were on our way back to Pembrokeshire.

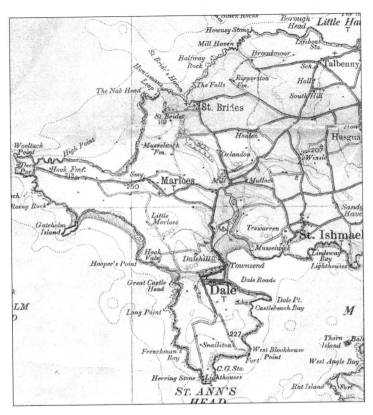

Reproduced from 1930s Ordnance Survey Map

# MARLOES

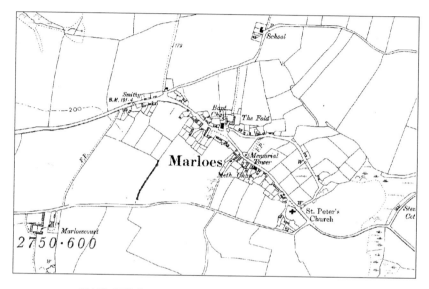

MARLOES from a survey of 1874 and revised in 1906

As we approach Marloes in January 1935 we have already crossed the tortuous and single lane Mullock Bridge, the only overland connection between Marloes and Dale with the outside world. From Mullock Bridge telegraph posts line the road to Marloes but telephones are as rare as cars on the road. Following a gentle valley through which a fitful brook wanders, the road swings round to the left and about 300 yards later, we pass Stembridge Cottages on the right before we arrive at the junction where we have a choice. We can take the left turn for Dale or the right turn for Marloes. For the moment we will take the left turn for a brief diversion which brings us to Philbeach Farm and its farmhouse furnished with an unusual Flemish chimney and attractive garden. Stanley and Annie James with their two children Esme and Tom, live here. Later Esme will hold a secretarial post in 10 Downing St when Churchill is Prime Minister.

Returning to the junction at Stembridge we now go straight on towards Marloes and almost immediately we pass the distinctive AA sign with its corporate colours of black lettering on a circular yellow disc telling us that it's 12 miles to Haverfordwest and 264 miles to London. A gentle ascent takes us to the first building in Marloes, the church. Before we enter Marloes village we will take another diversion by turning left just before the church and another gentle climb takes us past a house on the right where Eira Morgan lives. Continuing on this lane for 300yds we reach a lane on the left which leads to Little Marloes farm where Leslie, Eleanor and Kathleen Davies live. Later on, during our stay in Marloes, they are followed by Stanley Warlow and his family. Continuing straight ahead for a further quarter of a mile we pass Marloes Court Farm on the left. Here Frank and Claudia James live with their sons Peter and Michael. In a further 400 yards we find on the left a track leading down to Marloes Sands. Hardly anyone ever goes there but 60 years later it will appear in many picture postcards, calendar photographs of Beautiful Britain, Beach Guides, Walking Guides and tourism advertisements.

It's time to retrace our steps to Marloes, a name of Nordic origin. Mar as in the Latin and French related words, mare meaning sea and the Nordic Loe meaning tump. No wisecracks from the good folk of Dale please. The first building on the left is the parish Church of St Peter. It has a somewhat austere exterior and the interior is hardly more inviting. In the corner of the churchyard near the east gate stands the War Memorial where the names of the men of the parishes of Marloes and St Brides who had lost their lives in the Great War of 1914 -1918 are inscribed.

Names are usually recorded in alphabetical or chronological order but here the name of Captain the Hon Cecil Edwardes of the Scottish Horse and Tank Corps heads the list. Another man of Marloes had served in the Grenadier Guards. Nearly all the others had been in one of the several battalions of the Welch Regiment. There are 11 names from the joint parishes of Marloes and St Brides where in 1935, there are 201 and 85 names respectively on the electoral register.

No more than a track on the right opposite the church gives access to Glebe Lane where Tom Martin lives. On the left is a green lane which later will be overgrown. Further up the road on the left towards Marloes is a bungalow where Hughie and Ronnie Davies live. They are also in the cast. A line of single storey cottages continues on the left interrupted only by the Village Hall, a Methodist Chapel until about 15 years ago. The lone building on the right is Marloes Clock which is enclosed by a low hedge. This is a charming building completed in 1904, the funds for which were raised by the Pembrokeshire Liberal Association in memory of the 4th Baron Kensington. Perhaps in life his lordship felt that the people of Marloes needed assistance to be more punctual.

Marloes in the 1930s

Almost opposite lives Dicky Davies who is keeper of the clock and a little further on, Tommy Reynolds lives in the left hand of a pair of semi detached houses. A few more cottages on the left and we pass on the right in turn, the other end of Glebe Lane, the entrance to the smallholding known as the Fold and the footpath to Marloes School and School House. Then comes the Baptist Chapel and next to it lives Lydia Codd. On the left is the compact Green with cottages on two sides. Hugh Edwards lives in one of them. Continuing on the left we are now in the Square with neat cottages on two sides and a shop cum Post Office. In the top right hand corner, a little back from the Square, live Stanley, Iris and Thelma Morgan. In the centre of the square stands one of the three pumps which supply the village with water

The Village shop and Post Office

Continuing on our way in a north westerly direction we now have a gentle climb passing cottages on both sides of the road. On the left and a little off the road lives Kenny Thomas whose life was later cut short by a road accident in Milford Haven. A little further up the slope, but now on the right are more houses, in one of which Jim Thompson lives. Later he went to sea as a wireless operator. After that there is a grassy triangle from which a lane leads to the School and School House. Another track from the triangle leads to the Scales' farm at Musselwick. Beyond these tracks and just off the grass triangle is the blacksmith's forge where George Harries plies his trade. His forge gives out plenty of warmth and as boys we are keen to receive his wisdom on cold or rainy days. For some reason he always seems pleased to see us. As the gradient eases the only houses to the end of the village are on the left, one of which is a small wooden bungalow where Emma Edwards lives. She has a severe congenital deformity and has been confined to a wheelchair since she grew too big for a pram. Nevertheless she manages to keep herself busy by knitting high quality crochet.

Very shortly the village ends quite abruptly. Just beyond the last house on the left is a footpath to Marloes Court. Over the next mile or two there are a few farms and just one house on the left at Murchin where Commander Moore lives with his wife and daughters, Veronica and Islay. Commander Moore is ahead of everyone else in the area because he has his own supply of electricity from a petrol driven generator. A little further on the left side is Trehill Farm where James and Clara Codd and their family live. Almost opposite Trehill a track leads to East Hook Farm and about half a mile further and on the right is the track to West Hook Farm. The lane soon ends with a steep drop down to Martin's Haven, perfectly sheltered from the South West and here the fishermen keep their boats. In a shallow valley, protected by the higher ground of the Deer Park, is the cottage where Reuben Codd lives with his wife, formerly Betty Sturt.

To the north of Martin's Haven are St Bride's Bay and the Dewisland peninsula, the northern arm of the Bay with its principal communities of Solva and St David's. Roughly half way round St Bride's Bay at Newgale is the southern end of the Landsker, an invisible boundary which even as recently as the 1930's divides the Welsh speaking north from the English speaking south.

Travelling due west from here on an imaginary line  you clip the southern tip of Ireland and after that, there is nothing but 2000 miles or so of Atlantic Ocean. The next land you meet is the northern tip of Newfoundland.

Martin's Haven

Throughout this tour we have seen no more than a few trees leaning away from the prevailing south westerly winds. We might have seen a horse and cart but it is unlikely that we met a single car. Perhaps a couple of people were chatting outside the shop in Marloes and a lady was fetching water from the pump in the Square. Maybe there was an old man leaning over his gate and we might have seen a man on his bicycle on his way to his fishing boat at Martin's Haven. On a week day in the growing season we would almost certainly have encountered the roadman whose job is to cut back the luxuriant hedgerows of the parishes of Marloes and St Brides, his only equipment a billhook.

. . . . . . . . . . . . .

We moved to the School House at Marloes in 1935. The school was partly funded by the Church in Wales, its official title being Marloes N.P. (Non Provided) School. It was situated rather unpredictably a good 5 minutes' walk from the village of Marloes (population of the parish about 300) and about 30 minutes' walk from St Brides which, excluding the long stay patients at the hospital, had a settled population of barely 100. The only explanation that I can think of for the location of the school was that there was a supply of potable water at this point on the public footpath between Marloes and St Brides. Perhaps it was some sort of compromise reached by the rector of the day for he had pastoral responsibilities for the parishes of St Brides (where the rectory was situated) and St Peter's, Marloes. Lord Kensington (whose family name was Edwardes) had owned nearly 4000 acres in these parts as well as parts of London W8 including Marloes Rd, Philbeach Gardens and Fopston Avenue, the latter two named after farms in the parish of Marloes.

If all this sounds rather grand the School House was anything but, standing with the school in windswept isolation. The nearest neighbours were the Thomases in the Fold at Marloes, 400 yds away. The School and School House were approached by little more than a rough farm track, in places deeply rutted and used by a farm cart as frequently as any other form of transport. Leaving this lane a footpath, across a field and through the yard of the Fold, provided a shortcut to the village.

The School House in 1935 had no main services which meant that water for drinking and cooking had to be hand pumped from a pump 30 yards away in the lane and this also supplied the school. A large water butt to collect rain water from the gutter's down pipe stood by the back door and was used for all washing and bathing. There were two living rooms, a scullery in a corrugated metal lean-to construction and 3 bedrooms, two of which had fireplaces.

Water was boiled on a Primus stove which burnt vapourised paraffin (kerosene) or on the open coal fire in the living room which also doubled as a toaster. In the absence of a piped water supply, wash day must have been a particularly laborious operation for my mother as it would have been for every other housewife in the village. The lack of electricity meant that labour saving devices like a washing machine or a vacuum cleaner were not available either. Housekeeping in Marloes must have been hard work.

Pale yellow light was provided by paraffin oil lamps of the kind you see exorbitantly priced in bric a brac shops. An Aladdin lamp with its fragile mantle standing over a circular wick provided a much brighter yet softer light for reading. Very small paraffin lamps were used to get from room to room. Replenishing the oil in the lamps was a twice weekly task in the winter. Sometimes a candle might light the way but measured progress was necessary or the candle would be blown out. Heating in the living room was by a coal fire and elsewhere by a portable Valor oil stove. When I contracted what was called a "chesty cough", which I did only too frequently in the winter, a coal fire would be lit in my bedroom. A paraffin stove provided the heat for cooking.

There was of course no indoor lavatory and a primitive outdoor alternative was thoughtfully situated some yards from the back door. It consisted of a wooden seat with a hinged lid above a bucket. In the days before Andrex, old newspapers came in handy. In winter particularly, cold draughts chilled the fundaments but they dispersed acrid odours only too persistent on calm summer days, when flies patrolled the airspace.

A "wireless", as the radio was known, was powered first by a rechargeable "accumulator" which needed recharging after just a few hours' use and so was used sparingly. Later a car battery was acquired.

This lasted a few weeks before it had to be laboriously transported back to the village for recharging.

One redeeming feature of the School House was that it stood in a good sized plot of a quarter acre. Thus the lawn was big enough for bat and ball games. There were herbaceous borders containing the usual mix of annuals and perennials, punctuated by fiery red hot pokers and a rockery colonized by cerastium. I learnt to ride a bicycle on the path around the lawn before venturing on to the rutted and treacherous lane. There was room for a highly productive vegetable garden which my father tended with great care whenever he was well enough. Dad was an enthusiastic composter and we received a cart load of farm yard manure every year from Mr Richards at Winterton. Perhaps its fertility was also associated with its proximity to the privy; its contents had to be disposed of somewhere. The soil, dark and easily worked had been cultivated for 50 years. There was a good supply of the usual garden produce, all available on the table just an hour or so after being picked. The first broad beans and new potatoes of the season, liberally coated with melted farm butter were simple but delicious treats.

. . . . . . . . . . . . .

The school, built in the 1860's, was 30 yards away and accommodated about 40 children aged between 5 and 14 from the parishes of Marloes and St Brides. My father was assisted by a lady teacher of whom there were two in the time that I recall - Miss Rouse and Miss Lanham.

The School and School House

The school consisted of one big room divided during lessons into two class rooms by a tall folding partition. The large windows were situated quite high up in the building, presumably so that fitful attention would not wander. In winter uneven heating was provided by two upright coal burning cast iron stoves, each about 3ft 6ins (1.06 m) tall and fed through an opening in the top which was closed by a circular iron lid. The tall metal chimneys provided additional surfaces to distribute heat. In addition there was a small cloak room. The lavatories were at the back of the playground and certainly there was no great temptation to linger there.

The school day started at 9 a.m. In the playground boys and girls would line up separately by broad age group in rows with one arm outstretched to touch a neighbour's shoulder as if on a military drill square in a procedure called "Lines". My father, with his huge appetite for music and looking for any possible occasion in which to introduce a musical background, would then precede the children inside to the piano where he would play Mozart's Turkish March or something equally stirring as we peeled off from "Lines" to march into school in a brisk, orderly and silent crocodile.

For morning assembly and special occasions, the partition would be folded back. As it was a Church school the rector, D.H. Lloyd would sometimes come and say a few words. "D.H." as he was known to many was widowed during the time he was rector here. He brought up his two young children, daughter Pat, and son David, with some assistance from his mother in law and his sister Kitty. In spite of all his difficulties he managed to radiate good cheer wherever he went. His successor Tom Griffith, according to the school Log, was a less frequent visitor.

After prayers and a hymn, the register would be called. The partition would be restored and then it was down to work, each to his metal framed wooden desk which consisted of a folding seat and hinged top with an integral inkwell. Under the lid exercise books, reading books and pencils were kept.

Reading was taught by phonics and word building. In a child's early years writing the letters of the alphabet and figures, and then doing simple sums or writing simple words, was practised on slate. The figure or letter would be drawn by another piece of slate about the size and shape of a small thin pencil. The use of slate, although it now seems primitive, was highly practical since after use the slate could be wiped clean by a damp cloth and used ad infinitum.

One cannot help thinking that it was a grievous mistake on the part of the educationists of the 1960's to be beguiled into thinking that reading was best taught by "Look read" methods which included flash cards. It is quite extraordinary that it has taken 40 years for them to recognize the advantage of learning phonetic reading in tandem with learning to write the letters of the alphabet. In all this time they have totally ignored the reinforcing effect of writing on reading and conversely, reading on writing. Children even now are sometimes taught to read at least partly by recognition of word shapes but surely they do not learn to write by remembering word shapes. The abacus was used to teach counting and basic addition and subtraction before progression to "sums" on slate and thence to pencil and paper. Finally in the higher standards (forms), a pen would be used. This consisted of a replaceable metal nib on a wooden holder and required frequent replenishment from the inkwell.

The times tables - "one two is two, two two's are four" and so on were learnt up to twelve times by rote. The table would be written on a blackboard and the whole class would sing out as the teacher indicated each multiple in the table. The next table would not be attempted until the previous one had been mastered by all. This daily exercise must have taken some time, perhaps 2 years, to progress from two times to twelve times. We all engaged in this since we enjoyed the sense of participation which it gave and to which our friends, the educationists, attach such importance. Eventually even the most limited would instantly know that 6 x 9 was 54, 9 x 6 was also 54 and that 42 divided by 6 was 7. Here again the educationists have failed two generations of schoolchildren by abandoning learning by rote. Mental arithmetic was considered very important and simple calculations were as quick as any calculator.

At about this time Tom Martin and Jack Rayner were attending Haverfordwest Grammar School whilst Pamela Mactaggart attended Tasker's High School, all as weekly boarders but like other parts of rural Britain there was no strong tradition of secondary education in Marloes. Nevertheless I feel quite sure that very few, if any, pupils except the most seriously limited left elementary school without a good grasp of the 3 R's.

Apart from arithmetic, reading and writing there would be a variety of lessons in nature study, a bit of geography - "People from other lands", early history with stories like Romulus and Remus, Scripture, drawing and, always close to my father's heart, singing. Later "Musical Movement" with Ann Driver came over the radio from the BBC. At playtime in the mid morning each child would have a drink of Tuberculin tested (T.T) milk and dinner time meant sandwiches. It was only later, as a result of a wartime initiative, that school dinners were provided. After dinner there would be half an hour in the playground. Then at 1.30 it would be Lines again and another march to our desks to the rousing rhythm of Mozart followed by a return to lessons in less demanding subjects and organized games. The school day finished at 3.30 p.m.

Great importance was attached to games and to music as well as the 3 R's. This provided my father with another outlet for his enthusiasm for musical matters and I remember his efforts to set up a recorder group. In the late thirties, public as well as private finances were severely strained as a result of the Depression of the early thirties so there would have been no funds from the Pembrokeshire Education Authority to buy musical instruments. Pembrokeshire's farmers, easily the most important element of the local economy were having a particularly difficult time so they were not able to help very much either. My father's solution was to make the recorders himself fashioning them out of bamboo and corks, the finger holes being burnt out at carefully calibrated intervals with a hot poker. He constantly strove to create an environment in which appreciation of what he called "Good Music" would develop in his pupils by some sort of osmotic process.

Occasionally there were film shows which had educational value. These were shown by the Education Authority projector which circulated round the schools, the films silent apart from the hum and clatter of the projector. An entry in the school log in October 1939 tells us that the films that day were "So this is London", "Animals in their home" and quite extraordinarily for that time "A fishing trip round the coast of India". Educational subjects were lightened by films with Harold Lloyd, Will Hay in his role as schoolmaster and Charlie Chaplin.

Facilities for games, as one might expect in a small school in the difficult financial climate of those years, were pretty meagre. There was an unsurfaced playground but no playing field in the modern sense. We were however able to use part of a field, no more than uneven meadow, beyond the garden of the School House. Here we would play mixed games like Rounders, a simplified form of Baseball as well as improvised games of football and cricket. The sides would be picked by the two oldest boys, the captains, choosing alternately. In football two teams of 5 would play, coats serving to mark the goalposts. In cricket one batsman at a time defended his stumps and a single stump marked the bowler's end. The other members of the batting side would augment the fielding side. The school log in 1935 tells us that "a cricket outfit for the school was donated by the Hon Mrs Koe". Presumably she was a married daughter of Lord Kensington.

Each year the senior girls were joined by their counterparts from Dale for cookery lessons from a peripatetic Domestic Science teacher who would be in the school for 6 weeks. I cannot recall any comparable provision for the older boys until the early part of the war when some practical gardening as an extension of the "Dig for Victory" campaign was undertaken in part of the field previously used for games. This was a Government inspired drive to encourage householders to plant vegetables rather than flowers in their gardens. Home grown food not only improved the diet of the population but freed up valuable space in the merchant fleet for the transport of war materials. In 1943 over 1,000,000 tons of vegetables were grown in gardens and allotments.

The school, although it had enough books to go round for formal teaching, did not have a library. Instead a consignment of books would be circulated each term and delivered in a padlocked wooden crate from the Education Authority Offices in Haverfordwest. There might be 40 or 50 books to cater for a range of ages from 8 to 14.

Apart from occasional visits from the Rector the only extra curricular event that I can recall was an annual visit by a Mrs Pickrell from the Temperance Union who toured the schools of Pembrokeshire to warn us of the Evils of the Demon Drink.

The school log tells us that attendance figures were normally around the 95% mark although when the weather was stormy there would be many absences from the morning session. At other times the school would be closed early so that children, some of whom lived a mile and more away, could get home before dark. It was not until some years after the war that Marloes enjoyed the convenience of street lighting.

In March 1935, attendance fell to 28% due to an epidemic of Chicken Pox and in the following November the school was closed because of a measles epidemic when the attendance figure was 57%. There is a poignant entry in the school log at this time. One of the youngest pupils, 5 year old Grace Scale of Musselwick Farm, had died of a form of "meningitis following measles". In the days before immunisation, epidemics like measles and whooping cough swept through a community with devastating results. Perhaps it was no coincidence that the Rector came to the school the following day.

A few months later there was a 'flu epidemic when attendance figures dropped to 14 (about 33%).My father wrote "I intend to keep the school open as long as possible as those who are well are under my supervision and I take great care to see that both warmth and fresh air are obtained".

It wasn't only illness that affected attendance and the log in1936 states that there were many absences when "the weather was good for threshing" and in 1937, "many farmers experiencing labour shortages". Many of the absentees would have been boys of 12 or 13 who within a year or two would probably become farm labourers or work on the family farm themselves. It was a forerunner of work experience.

School holidays were much shorter in the 30s, the School summer holiday being a little over 4 weeks. In 1935 for example, the summer holiday started on 2nd August and the new school year started on 2nd Sept. The Christmas holiday was barely one week. To compensate for this there were frequent one day holidays as well as mid term breaks. The school log tells us that among other holidays in 1935 there was a "Manager's holiday to enable attendance at St Bride's Harvest Festival". There was also an annual holiday in July for Marloes Fair and a holiday in October for

Portfield Fair in Haverfordwest. After a short observance of St David's day on the 1st March, the rest of the day was a holiday.

I have no recollection of little Grace Scale's death from measles in March 1935. I was not yet 5 and did not start school until the following September. My parents presumably did not discuss this sad event in my presence. One incident, however less than a year later, created an indelible impression on me as a sensitive 5 and a half year old. In a fierce gale in January 1936 the Lowestoft trawler Sea Breeze (according to some authorities Shore Breeze) was blown ashore on the rocks at St Anne's Head immediately below, and invisible from, the Coastguard look out. A lighthouse keeper from a different position on the headland saw the lights of a vessel below him and raised the alarm. The coastguard, unable to stand up in the gale crawled along the cliff top on his hands and knees searching carefully but found nothing. He concluded that no more could be done to save the crew. 2 days later wreckage of the stricken vessel was found at Marloes Sands. A further search for bodies was begun but again nothing was found. A week later the crew of the Angle Lifeboat on their way back to the lifeboat station spotted an object high up on the cliff. This turned out to be the body of a survivor who, after a miraculous escape from the wreck, had managed to climb the near vertical cliff only to be defeated by an overhang of rock. He had died of exposure just 30 feet from safety. The tragic pathos of the event affected young as well as old.

. . . . . . . . . . . . .

Many people think that I must have had an idyllic boyhood and at times it certainly was. At other times, as an only child and the schoolmaster's son, I was lonely - not only physically isolated from the village - but in a sense "different" from my classmates because my father was the schoolmaster. In those solitary hours my companion was a golden haired cocker spaniel. "Ginger" had been marvellously trained because he always "wiped" his paws on the doormat whenever he came into the house and he would never enter a room uninvited but would wait patiently in the doorway.

He was a great comfort when I got into hot water with my parents, which happened occasionally. On these occasions I used to seek refuge and consolation with Ginger in a cubby hole under the stairs where I would inform him that he was "my only friend in the World". It seemed to me that with my arms around his neck, Ginger with his mournful expression understood perfectly. Unfortunately we were not destined to have Ginger for many years as he was already middle aged when he came to us and there was great grief at his demise. His successor arrived soon afterwards but was a quite inadequate replacement.

Winkle was a wire haired fox terrier whose early life had been spent in

Swansea. I'm not sure how he came to be with us but he had none of Ginger's character and I never really took to him in the same way. His stay in the countryside was quite brief. One day he started chasing sheep which the gentlemanly Ginger would never have dreamt of. The first time it happened he was called back and no harm was done, but soon there was talk of his having chased a sheep over the cliffs near Musselwick so Winkle's life in the countryside was short. He was soon on his way back to the city and there were to be no more dogs.

. . . . . . . . . . . . .

In the thirties pupils not going to grammar school stayed on at the Elementary school and finished full time education at 14. I cannot ever recall going home to tell tales about anyone but I suppose I must have done on one occasion, when I returned home in some distress. I had been bullied by a boy who was shortly to leave school. The bully was a big chap for his age whereas I was a particularly puny and delicate 7 or 8 year old. Flat on my back in the lane near the school, I was pinned to the ground by D who sat astride me with his knees over my shoulders. He got hold of my hair and proceeded to bang the back of my head against the ground two or three times as if my head was a door knocker. Perhaps I had been cheeky but life seemed quite unjust, being roughed up by someone nearly twice my age and twice my size. I don't recall being seriously bullied again after he had left school although there must have been one or two minor scraps as is the way with boys. I also recall deep hurt when I was called "Weasel", "Stoat" and most unusually "Vair" (to rhyme with wire), which I think is a Pembrokeshire word for the same animal. I had been unable to find this word or variation of its spelling anywhere until cousin Peter Davies recently found it in B.G. Charles' "The English Dialect of South Pembrokeshire (1982). The word is also found incidentally in South Glamorgan and County Durham.

The inevitable result of this separateness from my contemporaries was a determination to be at least as mischievous as they were and if possible more so. I had to earn what is now known as "street cred". This manifested itself for example in teasing Dicky Davies. He was the lame and aging caretaker of the village hall and the nearby village clock which was enclosed by a low hedge. Inside the hedge was strictly out of bounds so it was almost obligatory to trespass if there was any chance that Dicky might see us because he would shout and try to chase us. We knew we could always make a getaway because of his severe limp from a hip condition in childhood. Low level misdemeanours included knocking on doors then running away, or better still, when neighbouring door handles permitted, tying both handles together, knocking on both doors and retreating to where we could watch but not be seen, thus neatly inverting the old saw. It was now a case of little boys being heard but not seen. Other pranks involved fireworks and 3 or 4 of us chasing a poor donkey that occupied two small fields which had a communicating gap near the Beacon. Having chased the poor creature into the upper field one of us would remain behind whilst the others, after gathering some ammunition, took up position out of sight on the other side of the hedge in the lower field. When the ambush was ready the donkey was chased through the gap where it was greeted by a fusillade of sticks and stones. I like to think that our aim was poor and that I only participated in this delinquent and cruel behaviour no more than once or at the very most twice.

Our most serious misbehaviour was smoking cigarettes which, for boys of our age, were not easy to come by. My very first cigarette at the age of 8 was a Woodbine which came in packets of various sizes, the smallest a paper packet of 5 costing 2½ pence, the modern equivalent of which is 1p. I'm not sure who were my partners in crime on this occasion but it was probable that two of them would have been either Kenny Thomas or Hughie Davies and his young brother, Ronnie, better known as "Yattir". Yattir was a particularly cheerful soul and a popular figure who came by his nickname when he started school. When the register was called he could at first only manage "Yattir" instead of "Yes, sir". I understand he still goes by that name today and until recently kept a pub in Haverfordwest. I'm sure he would have been a genial landlord. In the village of Marloes, these were the boys I saw most of.

Having managed to raise with an assortment of ha' pennies and farthings the princely sum of 2½ d (1p) I led the way to the village shop and asked for 5 Woodbines "for my father". In spite of his peptic ulcer he used to smoke Players Medium Navy Cut which he usually bought in a round tin of 50. The shopkeeper must have known that we were up to no good but nevertheless she sold us the cigarettes. A few days' later my father went to the shop to replenish his stocks and was not at all pleased when he was asked by the shopkeeper, perhaps with a twinkle in her eye "How did you like those Woodbines that Lloyd bought for you on Saturday?" I have to say that, contrary to many people's experience, from the very first puff it was most enjoyable. There was no cough, no nausea, and no dizziness - just pure contentment. Very soon I was inhaling or as we called it, "taking it in" and the foundation was laid for a 30 year habit. I was hooked.

Fortunately we didn't have the funds to support our habit too often and smoking was always a collective act. We would share a cigarette passing it round. Sometimes if we had a stock we would smoke half a cigarette each and then expertly nip off the lighted end and store it for another occasion. A flat tin, perhaps an Elastoplast tin, acted as a cigarette case preventing the tobacco from drying out and the cigarette from being deformed, and was useful to keep these "butts" in as well as cigarettes. Fag ends would be collected and when there were sufficient, the tobacco would be extracted and a further cigarette rolled out of the remains. Sometimes we used newspaper for the wrapping but occasionally we might get hold of Rizla cigarette papers to produce a more refined smoke.

We had 3 ways of lighting a cigarette, the first being the orthodox England's Glory match which flared efficiently if struck on a dry stone. Another method on a sunny day was a magnifying glass which was also useful when we wanted to light a fire. The third method was using a piece of steel and striking it against a flint stone, the resulting spark sufficient to set the tinder (a piece of cloth impregnated with saltpetre held tightly against the flint) smouldering. When the tinder smouldered sufficiently it was held against the cigarette and after a few feverish sucks the cigarette would be lit and used to "give a light" to the others. I can't think where we got the saltpetre from but we used it a few times.

Smoking led to another difficult situation for my father a year or so after my first purchase of the 5 Woodbines. The episode of the cigarette butt must have tested him sorely. By this time I was in the "scholarship class".There were 5 of us, Joyce Griffiths and Gordon Rayner from St Brides, Stanley Morgan from Marloes, Peter James from Marloes Court and myself preparing for " the scholarship", later to become the 11 plus.

We were standing in a line in front of my father receiving a collective rebuke. Whatever the reason, I started to giggle, often my reaction when in trouble. In an attempt to conceal this totally inappropriate response, I hurriedly pulled a handkerchief from my trouser pocket to cover my face. Unfortunately as well as the handkerchief, out popped a cigarette butt which I was keeping for future recycling. It caught his eye as it rolled inexorably across the floor towards him. I had some quick thinking to do.

"What are you doing with this, boy?" he enquired none too calmly.

"I found it in the lane and was bringing it home for you, sir".

My poor father's face was a picture. I thought he was going to explode. Here was his 9 year old son, supposed to be an example to the other boys. First of all giggling when we were already in trouble. Then there was evidence of smoking cigarettes and as if this wasn't enough I had compounded the misdemeanour by suggesting that I was searching the highways and byways for cigarette butts to bring home to him. Unfortunately I never did get a chance to have a grown up discussion with him on this and other matters. He had a good sense of humour so I expect he had a quiet laugh about it later.

All 5 of us entered and passed the scholarship that year which considering the size of the school was no mean achievement. Another point that I would have wished to discuss with my father was why I was entered for the scholarship a few weeks short of my 10th birthday instead of the usual age of 11. Perhaps having read of my near delinquent behaviour you might think he wanted me out of his school sooner rather than later but it is more likely that he recognized the potential of the others in the group and he thought it might be to the benefit of both father and son if I went on with them.

. . . . . . . . . . . .

Apart from his family and his garden, my father's great passion was music. The piano, his pride and joy, was an upright Challen of dark mahogany. On the wall above the piano hung a black and white lithograph of his idol, Ludwig van Beethoven who frowned down at me disapprovingly. My feeling for him might have become a little more sympathetic when my father informed me that in his later years Beethoven had become deaf and had not heard a single note of his later compositions.

My father was a highly accomplished pianist. He could play a previously unseen score quickly and easily and could transpose effortlessly, first playing something in C, move seamlessly to D sharp and then perhaps to B Flat. He could extemporise and improvise weaving hints of other melodies with consummate ease. He would have made a good stand in for Joseph Cooper, the concert pianist, who entertained us so well in My Music on BBC2 in the 80's. As well as an excellent technique he played with great expression.

My father might spend up to an hour at a time at the piano. After five minutes of limbering up with scales and arpeggios, he would then play Chopin Preludes, Liszt Studies, Beethoven Sonatas or Bach Fugues. At the age of 6, I could hardly be expected to appreciate his skills as a musician but I can still recall in later years, performances of what seemed to be concert standard of many Beethoven piano works including the Moonlight, Apassionata and Pathetique sonatas and Chopin pieces, especially the dramatic and frenzied "Revolutionary Study". He had wanted to take a degree and pursue a career in Music but was dissuaded by his parents who disapproved of anything remotely suggestive of Bohemia. They thought that a music degree could never result in a "proper job". At the piano he would frown or shake his head, nod or bow as the mood of the music dictated or sway gently as he played a lilting melody. It was a great pity that he never had the chance to demonstrate his skills on a concert grand piano to a wider audience.

Dad lost no opportunity in exercising his musical skills outside the home and. he played the harmonium at St Peter's in Marloes and St Brides churches where he would extract musical miracles from these wheezy instruments, the bellows of which he pumped with his feet.

With his consuming appetite for music it's not surprising that he wanted to share this pleasure with his son. I have, probably through that same osmotic process that he hoped would inspire his pupils, developed an enthusiasm for classical music but I did not share it when he first gave me piano lessons. I used to marvel at his playing and certainly appreciated some of the melodies that could be enjoyed by a youngster but I had no wish to practice when I could be playing with Ginger. Better still on Saturdays or summer evenings there was the thought of going out to play with the boys in the village or going for a ride on my bike. Having failed to arouse in me any enthusiasm, my father wisely but regretfully allowed some respite from the drudgery of daily practice.

Later when an attempt to revive my musical education was made, it was no more successful and I reached no higher standard than a wooden performance of Schumann's " Merry Peasant" and a faltering Mozart's Sonata Facile (called in later years by the musical populists " In an 18th century drawing room"). A few years later there were further disappointments for him as I tried to play Jerome Kern's " The way you look tonight" , Hoagy Carmichael's wistful "Skylark", and Irvine Berlin melodies which, even my father agreed, had decent if inconsequential tunes. Much later on I bought the piano score of "Skyliner" a terrific popular swing tune of the 40 s and when I played it with reckless abandon he must have been very disappointed.

. . . . . . . . . . . .

Marloes Court was a mixed farm of about 250 acres, owned by Frank James and his wife, Claudia. It was 20 minutes' walk from The School House and south of the village. Mr James was a very industrious and conscientious farmer - you had to be to survive in those difficult days. Ordinary conversation with him often contained strong language which would bring a stern rebuke from his wife. This chastisement would result in but a brief moderation.

Mrs James came from Eglwyswrw in North Pembrokeshire. She had come to Marloes as a young teacher and taught in the village school until she married Frank. In the 30s the good folk of Marloes would refer to any place north of the Landsker as "Up the Welsh" so she, like my parents, came from "Up the Welsh". People from the north of the county on the other hand would refer rather disparagingly to the south of Pembrokeshire as "Down below," the last syllable rhyming with cow. Although Mr James and my father never hit it off particularly well, my mother and Mrs James were good friends. The Jameses had two sons, Peter and Michael and later on, a daughter Ann. Very occasionally Peter who was some months older than me, and Michael a couple of years younger, would accompany us with their mother to Marloes Sands for a picnic. In those days we would usually have this wide and picturesque beach with its many interesting pools to ourselves even on Bank Holiday weekends. Occasionally we would see other humans but these would be the crew of a Breton crabber anchored in the lee of Gateholm. As far as I know the crew never came ashore because they knew they would have a warm reception from the local fishermen. It was not illegal to anchor there but feelings ran high when the Bretons were about, illegally and greedily plundering the rich stocks of lobster and crab to which they had no right.

Peter was soon helping out on the farm. From an early age he took on responsibilities and showed a maturity far beyond his years, early hints of his love of farming and appetite for hard work. He handled a horse and cart or a guided a plough drawn by Bonnie and Bright, a fine pair of carthorses, like a veteran farm hand and took great pride in the resulting straight furrows. Peter much enjoyed driving his father's Case tractor which he also did with the ease of a seasoned hand. The tractor had metal wheels with flanges to provide grip on soft ground and used TVO (tractor vapourising oil) as a fuel.

In hay making and corn harvest I used to spend a lot of time at Marloes Court, always ready to "help". These operations entirely powered by horses, were certainly laborious. The hay would be cut by a mower and after a couple of days drying in the hot summer sun, it would be turned over mechanically by a swaffer. After another day or so the hay would be raked and deposited in clumps by a hay rake ready to be loaded on to the cart by pitchfork and taken back to the yard. Here it would be off loaded at the base of a huge pitching post and hoisted in a grab by a horse in harness to build the hayrick.

As the horse walked backwards the grab would be lowered to the ground ready to be reloaded. As a skinny weakling my job was leading the horse back and forth, allowing Peter to take on more grown up work and I much enjoyed my part in all this. The hayricks in Marloes Court were always perfect shapes with straight sides and neat right angled corners.

Later on in the summer I was able to get involved in the corn harvest, the cereals being mainly oats with some barley. The crop was cut by a binder, the stalks being brought to the cutter by a series of paddles which rotated like a windmill as the binder moved forward. When a suitable and adjustable quantity of corn had been cut, it was tied mechanically in sheaves and then deposited on the ground. The sheaves were collected by hand and stood up on their cut ends to support each other in groups of 10 or 12 to make a stook. After a couple of days a stook would be enlarged by the addition of sheaves from surrounding stooks to make a mow (rhyming with cow) of 40 or so sheaves. This made loading the cart more efficient and improved the drying of the grain before it was threshed. After a couple of days, the corn would then be taken in by horse and cart to the yard where the threshing machine, belt driven by the Case tractor, would separate the grain from the straw.

Part of the pleasure of "helping" on the farm was the delicious supper of home cured ham and real farm butter, salty enough to give a cardiologist a fit, on crusty home baked bread. Home made ginger beer washed down this feast. If there was no one about to interfere or let on I was able to sample some home brewed cider. On top of all this I was getting paid!

It was in the farm yard of Marloes Court that I had my first lesson in sex education with a practical demonstration albeit in an equine setting. I can't recall which of Mr James' mares was to be "served" but I remember watching this activity with enormous interest. The stallion, magnificently equipped for the task was, with his proud owner, on tour in the area. To my inexperienced eye he carried out his duties manfully.

I cannot recall the situation in Marloes when the war started but as we have seen pre war school logs referred to high rates of absence at harvest time.

*Over the country as a whole there had been a drift of agricultural workers from the countryside attracted by the higher wages and probably better housing available in the industrial towns and cities. By the spring of 1940, 30000 farm workers left the land to join up and half as many again to other occupations. In the summer of 1940 the Government through the Agricultural Wages Board instituted a minimum wage of £2 8s (£2.40) a week. One year later this was raised to £3 a week and raised again to £3.5s (£3.25) in 1943. To cover the shortfall in labour the Government started recruiting volunteers for the Women's Land Army.*

*By 1944 the Women's Land Army had grown to 80,000 mostly employed on farms but also in market gardens. Their uniform consisted of green jersey, brown breeches and stockings and a brown slouch hat. Later in the war the agricultural labour force was supplemented, after Allied battlefield successes in the Western desert, by Italian prisoners of war (P.O.W.s) who wore a distinctive uniform of brown tunic with a yellow circular patch on the back. In 1943 there were about 75000 Italian P.O.W.'s in Great Britain and there was a P.O.W. camp on the newly redundant Talbenny aerodrome. They would be transported each morning to the farm on which they worked and collected at the end of the day to return to their camp. Later on some of them lived on the farm where they worked.*

. . . . . . . . . . . .

The people of Marloes were pretty hardy folk not given to complaint. Those in work rarely took time off unless they were very poorly indeed. It was considered a sign of weakness to have to visit let alone call the doctor. The nearest surgeries were in Milford Haven (10 miles) and Haverfordwest (12 miles). In populated areas health insurance schemes were available to those working for an employer but there were no employers on this scale locally. Private health insurance schemes operated for people who could pay by weekly door to door collections but I have no memory of anything like this in Marloes. In this scattered population employment was often seasonal and it is unlikely that many of the households could afford even modest premiums. Most of the common infections were self medicated which meant a couple of aspirins or perhaps a poultice.

Dr Rice, our family doctor was a quiet softly spoken Irishman who lived next door to his surgery in Charles St, Milford Haven. When called he would normally visit the next day bringing with him a bottle of medicine, its nastiness only matched by its inefficacy. As often as not the patient, on low wages or unemployed, could not afford to pay his fee but Dr Rice always came. Sometimes there was a modest payment in kind.

There were two other doctors in Milford Haven who visited the area, one of whom was the ebullient "Bunny" Evans and a much older and austere man, H.O. Williams. Dr Evans made his reputation when, in answering an emergency call on St Anne's Head one stormy night, he had been unable to stand upright in a gale and crawled the last yards on his hands and knees to the Coastguards' houses to attend his patient. H.O.Williams was a crusty old sort who greeted most patients in his surgery with a grumpy "Well, what's the matter with you?" In spite of his peremptory manner he enjoyed a high reputation for his clinical acumen and had a good rapport with the old folk. Doctors from Haverfordwest also treated patients in Marloes but the only names I can recall were MacGeoch and George. Dr Middleton was the County Medical Officer of Health who examined children in school periodically. There were two nurses during our time in Marloes; the first was Nurse Price followed by the diminutive and ever cheerful Nurse Davies. Her uniform consisted of a dark blue dress, starched cuffs and collar reinforcing the appearance of brisk yet kindly efficiency. Nurse was a busy lady combining the roles of District Nurse, Midwife, School Nurse, and Health Visitor as well as tending to minor medical matters. She lived in a Pembrokeshire District Nursing Association house in Glebe Lane.

I was a particularly sickly specimen. I seemed to go down with whatever bug was going the rounds in spite of daily doses of in turn, Cod Liver oil, Halibut oil capsules, Minadex and Virol. Tonsillitis was a frequent visitation. At other times a simple cold would be followed by a cough and a wheeze as it "went down on the chest". I cannot recall any of the epidemics mentioned in the School Log but I well remember days and particularly nights, coughing and wheezing away in my draughty bedroom, still cold in spite of a fire in the grate. In the years before antibiotics and inhalers there was very little in the way of effective treatment and an infection had to run its course.

Home remedies were ineffective and usually disagreeable. A product known as Lewis' Drops was highly regarded by my father's family who had great faith in its curative properties. This repellent concoction had been a household remedy in the mining valleys of South Wales where my father grew up. It was a tincture, the dose measured in drops from a dropper bottle. Among its ingredients were the minutest traces of Phenol. In the recommended doses this substance did no great harm but imparted a flavour very hard to describe but so disagreeable that the patient had to believe in its potency.

My mother on the other hand had a touching faith in the benefits of camphorated oil rubbed on the chest as it would "loosen the chest". Goose grease employed in the same way also enjoyed a reputation for easing the breathing but all too often my worried parents would ask Dr Rice to visit.

One occasion stays clearly in my memory when I had "congestion of the lungs". This was accompanied by a sharp pain even on shallow breathing and coughing was very painful indeed. A fire was lit in the bedroom and Dr Rice was called out that same evening. That night I was wrapped in a jacket of wadding impregnated with Thermogene which generated an intense heat. I cannot recall however, any relief from the pain to compensate for this additional discomfort.

In June 1936, my father's peptic ulcer perforated and even today this is a serious matter but with antibiotics and intravenous fluids in addition to surgery one would expect the patient to survive. In 1936 it was a matter of "touch and go". Dad was admitted to the Pembrokeshire County War Memorial Hospital at St Thomas' Green, Haverfordwest and was fortunate to be admitted under the expert care of Mr Gillam. The perforation was repaired and the abdominal cavity drained and after some days in a critical condition, he began to improve. He was able to return to work at the end of the summer holidays. A bank overdraft was negotiated to pay the fees but the financial costs of this were a heavy burden for years afterwards.

A year or so later I was beginning to lose quite a lot of time from school with "colds on the chest" and bouts of tonsillitis. In an attempt to improve health, appetite and mouth breathing, my tonsils and adenoids were removed in a clinic in North Road, Milford Haven. The clinic was in a building indistinguishable from its neighbours in a terrace of largish houses. I remember the doctor placing a gauze mask over my face and sprinkling chloroform over the mask. I think the man who put me under was the man who removed my tonsils, the anaesthetic presumably being continued by a nurse. She must have done her job well because my next memory is of a fire in my throat. An hour or so later in an attempt to cool things down my parents brought me some ice cream which remained in its proper place for just a minute or two before leaving through the same fiery passage. I came home the same evening.

P.C. MacTaggart was the custodian of law and order in our early years, followed by P.C. Ben Williams. He lived in the police house at Mullock Bridge and from here he kept an eye on the extensive territory of Marloes, Dale, St Brides and St Ishmael's using a bicycle to get about. It was clearly a law abiding community for the most serious offences at Rhoose Petty Sessions were riding a bicycle without lights and being drunk and disorderly. Very occasionally a case of assault and battery might be heard. The Western Telegraph and the West Wales Guardian, the two weekly local papers reported in infinite detail the circumstances of an offence including a summary of the evidence as well as a defendant's submission. It was just as well that it was a crime free area for the policeman carried out a multiplicity of duties including the supervision and certification of sheep dipping. He would also put in a magisterial appearance at occasions like a Social in the Village Hall where he would stand in the doorway, thumbs hooked in breast pockets. Invariably he would be offered a cup of tea and perhaps a bloater paste sandwich. He would certainly be on the scene to have neighbourly chats with all and sundry at Marloes Fair.

. . . . . . . . . . . .

The principal source of home entertainment was the radio and came to Marloes via the B.B.C. transmitter at Droitwich in the Midlands. Even though Marloes is situated in open country without any obstructing high ground for miles, the reception was never better than indifferent. A single BBC network broadcast regional contributions from Scotland, Wales and Northern Ireland.

Children's programmes of very high quality were broadcast in Children's Hour every weekday at 5 p.m. It was introduced by the warm and much loved voice of David McCullough as "Uncle Mac". Such was his appeal when he signed off saying "Good night children . . . everywhere", I was sure that when he said everywhere he had certainly not forgotten Marloes. The weekly serial that I enjoyed most was "Toytown" in which the Adventures of Larry the Lamb by S.G.Hume Beaman were related. Uncle Mac played Larry and baa-baaed to great effect. Other wonderful characters were Dennis the Dachsund and Mr Grouser who at least twice in every episode loudly exclaimed "IT'S DISGRACEFUL . . . IT OUGHT NOT TO BE ALLOWED".

There were some programmes that we all listened to. There was a dispensation to stay up to listen to "In Town Tonight" at 7.30 every Saturday night just after my bath (a weekly event in a galvanized metal tub, in front of the fire in the winter) and immediately followed by "Music Hall". This variety show typically consisted of a couple of comedians, a singer or two and perhaps a ventriloquist, an impressionist, a harmonica player or a violinist like Stephen Grapelli.

I recall one evening when Max Miller, the "Cheeky Chappy" and notorious for his risqué jokes, came out with an outrageous double entendre which even today, nearly 70 years later, would raise eyebrows and cause callers quite reasonably to jam the B.B.C. switchboard. I think that my parents hoped that the joke had passed completely over my head and not wishing to show embarrassment I stared fixedly ahead avoiding any sidelong glances. I have an idea that thereafter my father had a close look in the Radio Times every week to make sure that Mr Miller was not appearing in the forthcoming programme but he need not have worried. The BBC "rested" Miller for some years after that broadcast.

Another hour long programme eagerly awaited during school holidays and latterly in term time was Ronnie Waldman's "Monday Night at Eight" which included comic sketches and songs by Elsie and Doris Waters (sisters of Jack Warner) who played two characters, Gert and Daisy. The show also contained a short 5 minute murder mystery with a liberal sprinkling of clues and a red herring or two, the solution being given the following week. In these sophisticated days it would be regarded as laughable but I found it entertaining.

Sport, particularly Welsh rugby was keenly followed by father and son. Vivian Jenkins, Claude Davey, Wilfred Wooller and Haydn Tanner were our heroes. Commentaries were given by Captain Teddy Wakelam and to assist listeners to follow the course of the game, the Radio Times published a plan dividing the field into 8 areas labelled "A" to "H". While Wakelam would be describing the play, a soft voice in the background would be heard form time to time placing the location of the scrum or line out by interjecting a letter so that the listener would know the position of play. Great was the rejoicing when Wales won as they sometimes did.

Another sporting occasion I remember was the World Heavyweight Boxing Championship in New York in 1937 between the holder, Joe Louis and the Welsh challenger Tommy Farr. Because of Farr's involvement, interest in the fight was unprecedented throughout the whole of the U.K. I was woken at 2 a.m. to listen to the commentary with rapt attention. The outcome was disappointing because although Farr was the first opponent to go the full 15 rounds with Louis, he was narrowly defeated on points. The sound quality of the broadcast was poor with low intensity roars, crackles, whistles and hisses that were picked up as the radio waves crossed the Atlantic, further impairing an already indifferent reception.

Carefully following the news in 1939 could certainly not be counted as entertainment but it is appropriate here to recall the situation leading up to the start of the war. My parents like every one else who had a radio in Britain anxiously awaited the 6 o'clock news every evening as Hitler invaded first Czechoslovakia and then Poland. An ultimatum issued by the Prime Minister Neville Chamberlain to Hitler to withdraw his troops from

Poland before 11 a.m. on Sunday 3 September was ignored. I remember sitting at home listening to the grave statement that the ultimatum had been ignored and that war had been declared on Germany. The next day we were in George Harries' blacksmith shop to hear what he had to say about it. Although my father had first hand experience of trench warfare in the Somme and was wounded just before Armistice Day 1918, he never talked about it. I don't recall that there was any great display of emotion. If anything, perhaps there was a sense of relief that what had seemed inevitable for so long had now come to pass.

As the war progressed the National Anthems of all the Allies were played on Sunday evenings before the 9 o'clock news. The news was followed by a series of morale boosting talks by the revered writer J.B.Priestley called Postscripts. Ravel's Bolero was also frequently heard as the war progressed as was the drum beat of dot, dot, dot, dash - the Morse code for V standing for Victory.

Radio comedy played a big part in sustaining morale in the war. Tommy Handley's weekly ITMA (" It's that man again") was the most popular show with its catch phrases from the German spy "Funf" and the charlady "Mrs Mopp" who used to ask that old soak, Colonel Chinstrap "Can I do you now sir?"

The cinema played little part in village life, the nearest cinemas in Milford Haven being the Astoria and the Empire. In Haverfordwest there were the County Theatre and the Palace. The only bus of the week left Haverfordwest at 4 p.m. so I didn't see many films. The first film I saw was "Snow White and the Seven Dwarfs" and the second film was a treat after sitting the Scholarship exams, "Gungha Din" in the County Theatre in Haverfordwest.

. . . . . . . . . . . .

Social life in Marloes was mainly based on Whist Drives and "Socials", held in the village hall or sometimes in the school with contributions from enthusiastic locals perhaps playing an accordion or singing a song. There were the usual party games, spinning the plate and musical chairs - the music supplied by Dad at the piano, tantalising the contestants with changes of tempo. He would accompany community singing, prefacing the main tune with improvised flourishes and shifting to a different key before finally launching into the main melody smiling all the while. Doing the Lambeth Walk and the Hokey Cokey were favourite dances. I also recall a performance at the school by someone who extracted an extraordinarily good tune from a wood saw and violin bow.

A trick called the "Aeroplane Ride" proved very popular at one Social. Two or three volunteers were offered an aeroplane ride but they were destined to be victims. Taken out of the room, they would be tightly blindfolded. In the meantime four men would be called out to hold a rigid board at its four corners. The volunteer would be escorted back to the board on which he would stand with his hands resting on the shoulders of one of the lifters. On being told to lift the lifters would slowly bend their knees and bodies until they were kneeling on the floor. By this time the victim sensed that he was at least three feet off the ground when actually he was only three inches. He would then be told to jump. The sight of the victim instantaneously but safely landing on the floor produced gales of laughter but the victim could only manage a rueful smile.

The Harvest supper was another happy occasion when the good ladies of the parish in a highly organized effort prepared tasty ham sandwiches, paste sandwiches, cakes, buns, blancmanges, jelly, tarts and all manner of good things. Shrove Tuesday with pancakes was also enjoyably observed. Once a year there would be a parish fete with raffles and stalls of various kinds. One raffle prize I remember was given by Gracie Fields to whom my father had written asking her to donate a prize. It was just about the time that the war started and Gracie who had been a very popular singer had begun to lose some of her fans following her recent marriage to an Italian. She was best known for her song "Sally". She donated a perpetual desk calendar. I don't recall who won it but my father kept her gracious note which unfortunately got mislaid when we moved house in 1948.

Marloes Fair was a modest but festive occasion held on the Green every year in the first week of July. It must have been an event of some antiquity for in his book "Who was Tobias Codd?", J.W. Evans reveals that one of the important Codd family "sold his wife at Marloes Fair for one shilling". Unfortunately we are not given a year for this unhappy transaction. In 1936 there were swings, various stalls and sideshows but no roundabout and certainly no dodgems. In spite of hard times there were always plenty of onlookers with their children from outside the parish for they had long been saving up for this occasion.

Highlights of the pre war years, the Silver Jubilee of King George V in 1935 and the Coronation of King George VI in 1937 were enthusiastically celebrated. As well as the usual spread of good food and soft drinks, there were the usual events for different age groups and sexes - egg and spoon race, 3 legged races, throwing a cricket ball and of course a tug of war. Both teams consisted of some very fine physical specimens whose muscles had developed from years of heavy physical work on the farm. On both occasions a commemorative mug was presented to every child in the parishes.

This enthusiasm for delicious spreads suggests that I was a good trencherman but for 2 or 3 years I was nothing of the sort, nearly driving my mother to distraction. Jam sponge was fine and so were jelly and blancmange but eggs, meat of any kind, cheese or vegetables were not for me. I recall attempts to dawdle over food by making roads through mashed potato heaped up to represent mountains and hills. I must be one of a very select few whose eating problems were cured by a piano tuner.

We were having our midday meal, and judging from Mum's reaction, even more informally than usual. I had been as dilatory as ever in my eating, employing the usual delaying tactics when Mum saw Mr Backhouse, the piano tuner, pass the window on his way to the front door. In other words we were "caught on the hop". There must have been extreme urgency in Mum's voice and alarm on her face as she exclaimed, "Golly, there's the piano tuner". Whatever it was, my parents registered the effect on me as I immediately proceeded to gobble down my food at a rate that I had never achieved before even with my favourite food. Ever afterwards if I was messing about at the table, dawdling, stalling, diverting attention or whatever, the threat of sending for the Piano Tuner was immediately effective and immensely gratifying to my worried mother as she watched me eating up my greens.

I don't know why Mr Backhouse held such terror for me and later on I grew to enjoy his visits. He was a smallish man but a larger than life character who kept a music shop in Milford Haven. He was well known for his laugh which came readily. He would throw his head back and release a cascade of guffaws, sounds to be heard to be believed. After he had completed his first descent of the scale he would quickly regain his breath before launching on his next arpeggio. This would go on for three or even more cycles. If you can think of the "Laughing Sailor" at fairgrounds and on seaside piers, that was Mr Backhouse's laugh.

. . . . . . . . . . . . .

The parish of Marloes had a population of 300 or so in 1935 and here might be the time to have a quick look at the names on the electoral roll in that year. There were 25 bearing the name Davies and a concentration of the much less common name (nationally) Edwards of whom there were 24. 12 Codds and 12 Warlows were the next commonest names. A duplication of Christian names was also not unknown, there being for example two George Davies, two Mary Ann Davies and two William Davies. D.H.Lloyd the jovial Rector used to enjoy relating the names of no less than three contemporary Willie Edwards in earlier years. They were distinguished by a very Welsh method, so it was "Willie the Church", "Willie the Top" and "Willie Trousers". One cannot help speculating how the last named came by his unusual soubriquet. Did he sport plus fours as my father sometimes did (yet another source of deep embarrassment for me) or was he perhaps caught somewhere with his trousers down?

The village shop which, with the adjoining Post office on the Square, supplied the basics. Here Alfred John and his wife, Margaret presided.

There was also a shop next to the Baptist Chapel run by a lovely old lady, Lydia Codd. I can't think it ever ran at a profit as business must have been painfully slow. Profitability was further impaired by her habit of always adding a few more toffees or whatever to the carefully weighed order. There was very little pre packaging in those days and most sweets were stored in glass jars. Only chocolate and sherbert, a powdery confection aspirated by a tube from a paper bag, were pre packed.

The Baptist Chapel and beyond it Mrs Codd's shop.

Meat was sold from Fraser James' van which came to the village from Milford Haven every Saturday. Bread was also sold from a van which came twice a week. Paraffin for oil lamps, primus stoves, heaters and cookers was available in the village, I think from the blacksmith.

For everything else it was necessary to go to Haverfordwest, colloquially known as "Haarrfat". Although Milford was the bigger town and slightly nearer, it lacked the range of shops offered by the County town, the administrative centre for Pembrokeshire. Haverfordwest was also home to a big cattle market. Some of the farmers and Commander Moore were the only car owners in Marloes. In St Brides apart from the farmers, Ted Rayner, father of Jackie and Gordon and manager at Kensington Castle, drove a Riley and the Rector's wife drove their Rover.

The commonest way of getting to Haverfordwest was by a bus which started out from Dale. The bus was a ramshackle affair, painted dark blue with seats for about 20. The door opened outwards by pressing down on a levered handle rather like a pre war car door. The passenger would close the door but if a free arm was not available, the driver would pull a leather strap to slam it shut. The service ran on Tuesdays and Saturdays leaving Marloes at about 9.15 a.m. and returning from Haverfordwest at 4 p.m.

The return fare was 2/6d (12½ p). I remember one embarrassing occasion when we were due to catch the bus and some minor mishap had delayed our departure from the School House, a brisk 5 minutes' walk from the village. There were no formal bus stops - it was a case of hail and ride. I was despatched to run ahead as fast as I could to ask the driver if he would "Wait for my father and mother" which he did without demur. My parents arrived within a minute or two but it seemed like hours and I can still remember the excruciating discomfiture of it all.

The bus groaned and rattled through what were little more than lanes picking up passengers here and there. One regular who used to climb aboard at Rosepool was a lady with a chicken or two and a basket of vegetables for the Market. The journey to the terminus at The Plasterer's Arms in Dew St took about an hour during which time there would be much chatter and local news would be freely exchanged.

On these shopping trips there might be visits to Tom Davies, "The COUNTY CLOTHIER" which is now "COUNTY CLOTHES" in High St. and which was a quite high class establishment. This might be to buy 232 grey trousers and shirts and scratchy woollen vests and pants which my mother insisted I wear and which itched interminably. The theory was that these would protect me from the endless succession of coughs and colds. Nearby was the biggest department store, T.P Hughes, which my mother might like to visit from time to time but the family budget was always pretty tight and seldom stretched beyond basic needs. Almost opposite T.P.Hughes was Pugh Davies the chemist whose window displayed jars of brightly coloured liquids. My father would consult him if he was having a bad time with his peptic ulcer. When his ulcer was really troublesome his only solid food for weeks would be Farex, a cereal baby food and here he would replenish his stocks. There was another very good reason to go and see Pugh Davies for his daughter had married the son of no less a person than the great Sir Hugh Roberton, conductor of the famed Glasgow Orpheus Choir and so it was a great opportunity to exchange musical news and views.

The shop that I always wanted to visit was the toy shop, McKenzie's in Victoria Place. It seemed to have a huge collection of Dinky toys - accurate miniature replicas of cars, lorries and buses, the cheapest of which cost 6 pence (2½ p today). It also sold sheet music. Father would visit the bank to cash a cheque and to reassure the manager that he was still about.

At lunch time we would repair to Miss Griffiths' "Tea Room", strategically placed in Victoria Place. The rooms were gloomy on the brightest days and although Miss Griffiths was really rather nice, a rather eerie atmosphere pervaded the whole place. It would have made a perfect stage set for a Victorian melodrama. The menu was pretty sparse, limited perhaps to curling sandwiches and stale rock cakes which probably had been sitting in the glass display case for most of the week. However, her establishment was conveniently placed and patrons could leave messages which Miss Griffiths passed on to relatives or friends. Best of all they could leave their shopping with her until it was time to make the wearisome return up High St to the Plasterers' Arms.

Apart from the fact that it was a pub I'm not sure why the Plasterer's Arms was the terminus for Marloes. All the shops were down the hill in High St, Market St and Bridge St. Somehow its location emphasised the remoteness of Marloes. Green's Motors' bus station serving Milford Haven, Broad and Little Haven and Tenby was conveniently situated near the Cattle market almost half a mile away. The railway station from where Western Welsh service operated to St Davids was a nearly a mile away. The weighed down shopper or the occasional luggage laden rail traveller to Marloes faced a stiff climb up High St before the sunlit and gentle gradient of Dew St was reached. Perhaps the real reason, the bus' lack of power to haul a load of shoppers and their shopping up the steepest part of High St, dictated its position - well above the most testing gradients. The progress of a bus load of returning passengers with the extra load of shopping was always laboured even on the gentlest incline. The Plasterer's Arms no longer exists but it was situated in or near the building which is now Haverfordwest Labour Club.

Theoretically the return journey left at 4 p.m but departure might be delayed for up to 10 minutes or more. Perhaps one of the driver's mates had inadvertently been delayed at one of the many pubs in town or news had been relayed by a more punctual passenger that "Mrs Davies is on her way". It was essential not to miss the bus as there wouldn't be another until the same time on Tuesday. The anti climax of the return journey might be slightly relieved by the presence of someone who, after a few pints of mild and bitter, now enjoyed the illusion that he had a fine singing voice which we might like to hear. From time to time a box of day old chicks chirping away added to the cacophony coming from singer, gear box, engine and bodywork. On a good day there would be the pleasure of a new Dinky toy.

The only other way of getting to Haverfordwest was by Tommy Reynolds' taxi, an elderly Austin 12, but this was expensive. I think it was 10/- (50 p in modern money) but others have remembered a price of 7/6 (37p) and only used in exceptional circumstances when the bus was impractical. Tommy was undoubtedly one of the characters of Marloes. He lived almost opposite the Clock tower and it was said that he owned several houses in Milford Haven. He also had a side line in buying rabbits locally and selling them in Haverfordwest. A likeable fellow, he had been married for a time measured in days if not hours and he was now a confirmed bachelor set in his ways. He was bald apart from a thin rim of hair just above ear level which appeared to be almost continuous with his bushy eyebrows. His speech was rapid - like machine gun fire. His defining characteristic was that every 10 or 15 words, his quick fire speech would be punctuated by the words "Like then" said as one word - likethen in much the same way that some people would say "y'know". A conversation with Tommy sounded like this: "Mornin', Mr Lloyd Jones, how are you to day likethen? Nice day. What time would you like to be picked up likethen"?

The story about Tommy which as boys we liked best and whose last line we often rehearsed, was of his return to Marloes with some of the merry young bachelors of the village after a night's drinking and carousing - very probably after Portfield Fair. In due course there was the inevitable and urgent need for relief. One can imagine their merriment as, bowling along, they wound down the rear windows to void their bladders into the passing hedgerows. Apparently, Tommy fully aware of these proceedings, half turned to his passengers and said "Now a joke is a joke likethen, but please to keep your cocks off the seat".

The big event of the year in Haverfordwest was Portfield Fair. It was a quite extensive affair and occupied the whole expanse of St Thomas' Green where hundreds of people in their best clothes milled about. It was held in October and lasted 3 or 4 days during which the pubs were open all day. There was the usual assembly of stalls and sideshows, swings, roundabouts and most exciting of all, dodgem cars. There was also a boxer who took on all comers. I think there was a modest prize for anyone who went 3 rounds with him. I went to Portfield Fair most years between 1935 and 1939 but never got to see the boxing.

By far the biggest occasion I can remember was the visit to Haverfordwest of the annual Royal Welsh Show in 1936. It was then a peripatetic event alternating like the Eisteddfod does now between North and South Wales. It was held on an area on the northern side of the Dale road which had at one time been part of Haverfordwest racecourse. For me it was a truly momentous day as I enjoyed my first milkshake (strawberry) and I saw an aeroplane for the first time. It flew low overhead but did not attempt any aerobatics. Its very presence ensured its place as the star attraction of the show.

One royal and ceremonial occasion that I attended as a cub member of the Marloes Scouts was a visit by the Princess Royal, the sister of King George VI, to inspect the Girl Guides of the 3 Counties in May 1939. The Girl Guides were holding a rally in Pembroke Castle and I'm not quite sure in what way the Boy Scouts were involved, perhaps it was to help fill the space in that large arena.

. . . . . . . . . . . .

Although there was no recognized football or cricket pitch in the village, the annual cricket match played between the men of Marloes and Dale was always a keenly contested affair. It was played on the field above the Green, the pitch a narrow strip of meadow grass across the least sloping part of the field. The farmer, Mr Warlow of Little Marloes, used it for grazing his cattle and there would be plenty of evidence of their recent occupation. The strip would be cleared of cow pats and the grass would be cut once or twice before the match. The outfield was left uncut and uncleared. I think there was a light roller.

When we lived in Marloes this local Derby provided another occasion when roles of father and son were reversed and father embarrassed son. Here I should say that the men of both Marloes and Dale prided themselves on their physical strength, hardness and ability to stand pain so who needed batting gloves, or pads for that matter? On a wicket where a ball might rise, keep low, shoot or turn sharply my father, who had been quite a keen sportsman in his fitter days, rightly thought he did. Equipment was pretty sparse - 2 or perhaps even 3 bats, stumps and bails, 2 or maybe 3 pads, 2 balls but no batting gloves. No refinements here of a new ball to be taken after so many overs or so many runs. The new ball wasn't really new at all and was only taken when the older one was lost in the undergrowth of the hedge.

Marloes batted first and as usual the opening batsmen and their successors at 3 and 4 had declined to wear pads. Dad was going in at number 5 or 6 and wickets had fallen quickly and he was not ready for such an early entry. Waiting for him to pad up there was a bit of sniggering by a couple of the lads who clearly thought that this was quite an unnecessary precaution and I felt deeply uncomfortable. Eventually the long wait was over and Dad strode to the crease and asked the umpire for "Middle and leg", by no means a routine preliminary in these fixtures, causing more sniggers. My discomfiture was complete when the first ball he received was a venomous shooter and in no time at all he was making his way back to the hedge which did duty for the pavilion and where his team mates and the solitary scorer looked on. His stay at the wicket had been much briefer than the delay resulting from his preparations.

These matches were low scoring affairs. An innings might last an hour but sometimes 45 minutes would be sufficient. Never was a match drawn because of lack of time. A total of 60 or more was most unusual, 50 was regarded as a good score and a winning total. As often as not it would be 30-40, the slow outfield impeding the few ground shots. It was not unusual for a bowler to return an analysis of something like 5 for 16 while few batsmen got to double figures. Occasionally a side might be skittled out for under 30.

One heroic figure was Willie Lawrence, 6 foot tall and more. He was no stylist but obviously had a good eye for the ball and on the occasions when his swinging bat connected, it was a certain 4 or more likely a 6. His stay at the crease was occasionally brief, usually productive but always spectacular. Often there would be no more than 22 men and boys at the game and so the batting side would provide the lone umpire. In these circumstances it's not surprising that decisions on lbw and snicked catches by the wicket keeper were sometimes controversial. There was no pub to repair to after the match but if the Lobster Pot had been in existence, Marloes cricket would have had many more home fixtures. There would have been football matches too but I have no memory of these.

. . . . . . . . . . . . .

In pre war days before continuous working became commonplace, Sunday was a quiet day over most of Britain. It was a day of rest for nearly everyone. Neither shops, pubs nor cinemas opened and transport services were greatly restricted all over the country. If life was pretty quiet in Marloes in the week, it was even quieter on Sundays. There was no playing in the road or on the Green. The cows had to be milked but there was no potato picking, haymaking or harvesting of corn. In traffic free Marloes the loudest sound would be the insistent sound of the single church bell tolled by Dicky Davies whose third responsibility in the village was as verger at the church.

After D.H.Lloyd's departure to Fishguard, the rector during most of our stay in Marloes was an unworldly and as I remember him, rather severe man called Tom Griffith. An Oxford graduate, known for his reserved attitude he possessed neither sense of humour nor ability to relate to his flock. He went around with a faintly puzzled expression, his nose slightly raised as if trying to locate or recognise the source of some vaguely familiar and slightly unpleasant smell. He seemed almost monastic except that he had a wife, Dorothy, who drove him around his scattered flock in their Rover.

To the best of my recollection, the morning Service was usually held in Marloes and the evening service at St Brides. There was an expectation that I would go to church at least once, usually in the morning to Marloes where needless to say my father played the organ. On fine summer Sunday evenings during school holidays I would have to traipse over to St Brides as well. Here Dad would also play the organ. It's a pleasant enough walk for an adult - about a mile across fields, a short section in a lane and then the best part, along a hedge from which the scent of honeysuckle wafted on warm summer evenings.

The Rector was reading the first lesson on just such a day. Rays of evening sun filtered through the windows and through the open door the sound of birdsong could be heard as the scent of honeysuckle drifted in.

Taking a service the Rector's delivery was quiet and rather monotonous.

As he was reading at the lectern a bird flew in. This in itself was quite a distraction but was soon to be followed by an even greater one as a cat strode in, tail erect, in pursuit of the bird which was now fluttering above the choir stalls vainly looking for a way out. The cat obviously meant business as he stalked up the aisle. It wasn't just the children who were distracted as smiles spread throughout the congregation. Mr Griffith however was anything but amused and the next part of the Lesson would have gone something like this: "And Moses called all Israel and said unto them, NEVER MIND THE CAT!   . . . Hear, O Israel the statutes and judgements which I speak in your ears  . . . NEVER MIND THE CAT!" … … the last instruction spoken with even greater urgency and volume … "In thy kingdom. . ." only to repeat what had now become a bellowed command totally inappropriate to this hallowed setting. After a few minutes the bird flew out and the cat seeing no prospect of a catch retired, no doubt to the relief of the Rector but to my intense disappointment.

If we went to church at St Brides  during the summer holidays, the evening service would usually be followed by an invitation to supper with John Young and his wife Meg, their son Monty, in his late twenties  and daughter Mary who in her mid twenties, cut an attractive figure. Mr Young as a young man had come down with his wife from Paisley in Scotland to manage the Kensington Estate. He was a colourful figure with a good covering of snowy white hair, a pink complexion, blue eyes and a broad West coast Scots accent. He suffered from asthma which sometimes prevented him from making a forceful point but only momentarily. A couple of squeezes on the rubber bulb of his inhaler, some coughing, a brief pause to regain his breath and he would continue.

As his lordship's representative it is unlikely that he enjoyed popularity but he was known to be scrupulously fair and conscientious and if not exactly loved he was highly respected. The Kensington Estate was wound up after the 14-18 war and the stately home of St Brides became a TB hospital. Mr Young became the proud and hard working owner of what had been the Home Farm, a considerable undertaking which later became known as Hill Farm. True to his roots Mr Young raised a dairy herd of Ayrshire cows, one of the first in the county to be milked by machine.

Supper with the Youngs', even though there no others of my age, was always enjoyable because they were the most hospitable hosts imaginable and Mrs Young was a very good cook. Afterwards there would be a ride home in their car and that too was a special treat. Other generous supper hosts were the Richardses of Windmill Park, their son Lawson and their daughters Gwen and Edna.

The family seat of the Kensingtons

. . . . . . . . . . . .

There were visits from relatives from time to time. Among our first visitors in 1935 were my mother's sister Hilda and her sons, Robin aged 5 and George was 3. Their father Jack Harries, Vicar of Llangedwyn in North Wales who had taken a Maths degree at Jesus College Oxford, had died at the early age of 35. Having lived in what was virtually a tied house, Auntie Hilda now in straitened circumstances had to find somewhere to live almost immediately. During this very difficult time her brother and two of her married sisters rallied round as families did without question in those days, and in turn accommodated her and the boys until the problem was solved when she found a house in St David's. Many years later Auntie Hilda was to marry D.H.Lloyd, Rector of Marloes and St Brides in our first years.

One special guest was my paternal grandfather. Granpa had spent most of his working life underground in a coal mine latterly as a deputy, the underground equivalent of a foreman. He had started in the pits of the Rhondda Valley. Trying to escape the industrial scene, he made an unsuccessful venture into chicken farming on the Cardiganshire / Carmarthenshire border. Unfortunately this venture coincided with the onset of the Depression which ravaged all the industrial areas of Britain and eventually he had to return to the pits, this time to Trimsaran in the Gwendraeth Valley.

As befitted a gentle and softly spoken pipe smoker he loved the

40

countryside and certainly enjoyed the country pursuits of shooting and fishing. During his stay at the School house he would shoot rabbits (delicious in a casserole) or catch fish off the rocks at St Brides'. It was reckoned that he seldom returned to the School House without a couple of fish or a pair of rabbits and in late summer there might be mushrooms as well as blackberries. Unfortunately as he was approaching a well earned retirement after a hard life, he was stricken with cancer. He succumbed before he could realise his lifelong wish to spend more time in the country. I was 6 or 7 when he died and so I missed the opportunity to hear his tales of life underground.

Going to stay with him however was not so much fun, particularly on Sundays. He was a deacon of his Baptist Chapel where nothing but Welsh was spoken. The singing was good but the long sermon, lasting up to half an hour and delivered with increasing emotions as the preacher's hwyl grew, bored me stiff. As I didn't understand a word of Welsh this was always a tedious hour or more and the only way I could think of to amuse myself was to count the number of times Granpa and another man, possibly another deacon of the chapel, would express audible agreement saying Odw (Oddoo meaning yes) or Nadw (Naddoo - no) as required and keeping the score of interjections. On a good night Grandpa might win 8 to 7 but there would be lower scoring but no less exciting times culminating in a 4 all draw.

My parents in an effort to increase the household income occasionally took in paying guests referred to as "P.G.s" who, for a modest charge, would have bed and full board. The only one I can clearly remember in Marloes, perhaps because she was a return visitor, was a dear old lady known in the family as "Miss Davies the Artist". She used to stay for a few days in the summers before the war. I do not have any of her work but she made a modest living from her painting of local scenes and teaching art. One less attractive feature was her liquid speech. She had a marked lisp and, unable to say her sibilants, dispersed a fine aerosol of saliva over those who, it might be said, were within spitting distance.

Another guest, although not a paying guest, was the Principal of St David's College Lampeter, Professor David. St David's College was an independent college mainly taking students intending to be ordained in the priesthood. Professor David came one weekend to stay with us when he was doing a locum for the Rector of Marloes and St Brides. On leaving he presented me with a beautifully bound and richly illustrated volume of Aesop's Fables suitably inscribed. Standing next to John Bunyan's "Pilgrim's Progress" in my bedroom it hardly presented an exciting prospect for an 8 year old. The Radio Fun Annual would have been much more to my taste. At that age I'm afraid I just didn't appreciate just what a fine gift it was and I no longer have what must now surely be a collector's piece.

With the outbreak of war came engineers and surveyors to build the aerodrome at Dale. Our first wartime guest was a cheery Lancastrian called Salt, a surveyor working for the contractors Sir Lindsay Parkinson. Wages for manual workers and drivers were very good although I don't think that many local men were able to get jobs.

The airfield became operational in the summer of 1941, the first unit a Polish Squadron of the R.A.F. which had been previously stationed in the North of Scotland. It formed part of Coastal Command whose duty was to patrol the Western approaches searching for U boats (German submarines) and enemy surface warships. So it was that Mrs Moisiewicz, the wife of a Polish pilot and a jolly lady, came to live with us for a short time. She had her own room and usually prepared her own food and she introduced us to one culinary delight which consisted of among other things chopped bacon and rice fried with onions - I wish I knew the recipe or could remember the name of the dish.

Although not a visitor in the social sense, the School House occasionally saw the sort of caller not seen today. The gipsy who called most regularly was Marjorie Lovell whose main selling line was clothes pegs. Her face was tanned and deeply lined by exposure to all winds and weather. She appreciated the cup of tea my mother invariably offered her - not that Marjorie ever needed any encouragement. The cup she had used was washed very carefully afterwards. My mother always declined Marjorie's offer to tell her fortune but we were never short of clothes pegs. "Johnny Onions", one of the many Bretons called "Johnny Onions", who came over from Brittany to sell ropes of onions was an annual caller. He seemed to do quite good trade and although I am not unduly enthusiastic about French commerce by and large, it's good to see Breton onion sellers back again.

. . . . . . . . . . . .

Holidays spent in hotels and touring in the pre war years were the prerogative of the well off. Even modest Bed and Breakfasts were out of reach for most people so family finances did not permit holidays away from home. Bank holidays were at Christmas and on Boxing Day, Easter Monday, Whit Monday and the first Monday in August when most industrial concerns closed down for a holiday week. Summer bank holidays provided the opportunity of a day trip to the seaside but that would be the extent of travelling. For these seaside excursions, parents would start saving up immediately after Christmas and as soon as that excitement was over the family would start saving for next Christmas.

In rural areas like Marloes, farmers rarely took a day off except to go to market. Even then there was the evening milking of the cows, usually to be done by hand, to return to after a day out. The summer months were the busiest times of the year, hay making and corn harvest going on from morning to dusk. In an effort to maximise productivity in wartime, Double Summer Time was introduced so that it was possible to carry on working until 11 p.m. on summer evenings. Farm labourers worked 6 days a week, glad of the chance of employment. Fishermen too would not be able to take time off in the summer months when the weather favoured their work.

As a schoolmaster, my father was in a much better position regarding holidays although there is a popular fallacy that teachers don't have anything to do out of term time. The holidays that teachers enjoyed to some extent compensated for the poor pay (£250 a year). Even so a teacher's income was handsome enough compared with manual workers' wages. In 1940 when agricultural workers' pay was raised, it was still only about £125 a year. To put this into perspective £1 in 1935 had the purchasing power of £40.72 in 1998. Using the index of Jan 1987 as 100, the long term price of goods and services was 4 in 1935 and 165.4 in 1999. In other words the price of goods and services had gone up 40 fold between 1935 and 1999. Fortunately wages have gone up by considerably more.

The arrangement for holidays in our family was that one family would visit another for a week or so and then the visitors would reciprocate as hosts. This arrangement worked particularly well for us as my mother's sister, Muriel, was married to another schoolmaster, Bryn Davies, Headmaster of Llanrhian, a village between St Davids' and Fishguard. They too had an only son, Peter who was just 3 months older than me.

I think I can safely say that I enjoyed staying with Peter at Llanrhian much more than he enjoyed coming to Marloes. For one thing Uncle Bryn had a car, a red Standard 8. Peter had a small billiard table, a dartboard, a bagatelle board and a Hornby O gauge railway set with a model of the Castle Class locomotive, Caerphilly Castle which I greatly coveted. He and his parents were splendid hosts and Uncle Bryn had a seemingly inexhaustible supply of jokes and puns. One I remember particularly when he was tidying us up in pre church inspections on Sunday morning. My hair was as ever the problem. I had a "cow's lick", my hair in the front standing up like a fan and even after being suppressed with water, it soon regained its rebellious vertical stance. "Lloydie", Uncle Bryn would say "your hair's like Heaven - there's no parting there". I can only recall one serious fall out which says a lot for Peter's innate good humour.

The weather it seemed was always fine and warm and picnics on the beach at Traeth Llyfn near Llanrhian or Whitesands near St Davids, where we would be joined by Robin and George, were routine events. If the weather by some mischance was not good enough for the beach there might be cricket with the wicket marked out on the garage door. If it was raining there was snooker, darts, bagatelle or "Dab Cricket", a pencil and paper game in which we would assume the person of our heroes. Peter was Maurice Leyland the Yorkshire and England batsman and I was L.E.G. Ames, the Kent and England wicket keeper/batsman, both of whose pictures we had each collected in a series of 50 cricketers on John Player cigarette cards. All this may sound as though we were "anoraks" but it kept two energetic 8 year olds fully occupied for hours on end on that rare rainy day.

An extra bonus at Llanrhian was that Peter had comics which I didn't have. My parents thought that A.J.Mee's Children's Newspaper would be "better" for me than the Beano, Dandy and the like. Later there was a modest relaxation and I was allowed the splendid Boy's Own Paper which promoted ideals of gallantry, derring do as well as moral tales, instructive articles and "How to. .".

Perhaps the best holidays were spent camping at Whitesands near St Davids where Uncle John and Auntie Nell would bring their family of David, Young John, Mary and Michael now living in Leicestershire. Peter and his parents were also campers and my parents and I would complete the group of bell tents usually set up just above the beach in an area supposedly the site of St Patrick's chapel. Robin and George were already living in St Davids so they joined in too. There would be swimming, games of cricket and football, fishing in the rock pools, and lots of fun building dams. Design and construction work of dams was supervised by Young John polishing his leadership skills which were put to use later when he became a subaltern in the South Wales Borderers in Burma in the immediate post war years. Of course the weather was always sunny and warm - except on one infamous occasion.

It was the year before my father bought a bell tent and we were renting a wooden hut in the burrows above Whitesands. It was hardly bigger than a beach hut but all was going well until one night, shortly after midnight the wind got up and soon a strong wind became a fierce gale. Although the hut was situated in a sheltered hollow it was not quite sheltered enough. The wind howled and the rain hammered down on the wooden roof. At about midnight there was much ominous creaking which grew louder and became continuous, followed by the cracks of breaking woodwork as the roof blew off. We were now exposed to the full fury of a force 7 or 8 and its accompanying deluge. I remember being carried down in the driving rain through the burrows where we sought refuge with Uncle John and his family who were on their usual site in their bell tent. Here the scene was also somewhat disconcerting as Uncle John and his family were sitting around the circumference of the tent keeping it on the ground, preventing it from taking off into the night.

Whitesands was the scene of a more dramatic situation two or three years later. It was the last evening of the family camp and the following day we would all be packing up - cousins Robin and George would be returning to St David's and thence back to boarding school, Peter and his parents to Llanrhian, Uncle John and his family to Billesdon in Leicestershire and us to Marloes where a frequently solitary life awaited. It was a rather dull breezy evening, the sea grey and uninviting, as we walked back from our picnic spot to the tents. Some distance along the beach a group of people were standing at the water's edge, looking out to sea and pointing. At first I didn't appreciate the reason for their interest but suddenly Uncle John took off his coat and then his shoes and socks. He had seen 30 or 40 yards out to sea a swimmer in difficulties. His sisters, realising what he was intending to do protested loudly, imploring him not to go. In spite of further cries calling him back, he ran into the surf and struck out for the casualty. He was a strong swimmer and eventually recovered a girl in her late teens. Unhappily his efforts were in vain. She was unconscious when he got to her and she could not be revived when he got her back to the beach. The end of the summer camp was always a bit of an anti climax but that year we were all particularly glum.

Uncle John was everyone's favourite uncle. His 5 sisters and their progeny all revered and treasured him. This was not surprising because he had a gentle authority that came from being quietly spoken and a placid temperament that never gave way to outright anger. His method was calm diplomacy accompanied by a twinkle and a smile. I don't think I was the only one of his nephews who wanted to bask in his approval. Uncle John was special in other ways too for it was not the first time he had risked his life to save another. Many years earlier he had dived into a canal in the Midlands to rescue a drowning person. Unfortunately that attempt was also too late.

He had seen action in Salonika in the First World War and soon after the Second War started he was back in uniform again, this time as an Army Chaplain. Later he was in the thick of things in the Normandy invasion. I'm sure there are still some "Uncle Johns" about but we could do with so many more. Much later on he was awarded a M.B.E. of which he was very proud, probably much prouder and certainly more deserving than many holders of yet higher honours, pop stars, placemen, jobsworths and time servers as many of them have been especially since May 1997.

. . . . . . . . . . . .

The outbreak of war on 3rd September 1939 brought an end to these carefree days. The Territorial Army had been mobilised and call up began for those men over 18 who had not already volunteered. On the home front gas masks had already been issued in the preceding weeks and food rationing was brought in.

*This was a successful attempt to prevent the shortages, higher food prices and racketeering which had so disfigured the country in the First World War. It was claimed that as a result of food rationing nutrition had improved for the average British worker. Everybody was issued with a ration book containing coupons for various staple items and a point system for the extras. It is worth recalling briefly the weekly allowances for various items:*

*Sugar 8 oz, (240 g) , Butter 2 oz, (60g,) Tea    2    oz,    (60g),    Cheese 1.5oz,(45g), Margarine 4oz, (120g), Bacon and Ham 2oz. (60G)*

*Meat was rationed by price - 1 shilling (5p in today's money) worth a week.    Other items like cereals, rice, tinned meat and biscuits were rationed by a points system, each person receiving 16 points a week. Additional allowances were given to men in heavy manual work.*

There was great uncertainty and anxiety and return to school after the summer holiday in 1939 was delayed to avoid concentration of children in any one place in case of enemy air raids. In the school log on 11 September 1939 my father recorded that the "School reopened. Gas masks carried by all the children and tests carried out". By this time the Local Defence Volunteers (L.D.V.) had been formed. It was the forerunner of the Home Guard which many years later was humorously recreated as the TV programme, "Dad's Army".

Soon anti aircraft and searchlight crews were stationed in the area and construction of a second temporary bridge began at Mullock Bridge. My father now 40 and not in the best of health became Air Raid Precautions (A.R.P.) warden for Marloes. After distribution of gas masks with demonstrations of how to use them and advice on how to protect windows against blast, his duties were twofold. Firstly like the villainous William Hodges in Dad's Army, he checked that the blackout was being observed and that no lights were showing which might assist enemy aircraft to know their position. He was conscientious without being officious and he used to patrol the village fairly regularly. In fact there was strict compliance everywhere and rarely if ever any infraction. He also had to ensure that the black out was observed by the few vehicles in the area. Car headlights in the 1930's were never very illuminating even when on full beam on the clearest night. Such light as they cast on the road ahead was now reduced to the faintest glimmer by a mask over the lens in which a  horizontal slit had been cut out to allow the passage of a feeble beam of light.

In the absence of a siren in rural areas, the warden's chief duty was to warn of imminent action of enemy aircraft by blowing a whistle. This responsibility required the installation of a telephone at the School House so that my father could be quickly informed of enemy activity. There were two levels of warning; a "Yellow warning" which indicated that enemy planes were somewhere over this part of the country and a "Red warning" indicating that enemy action was expected in the area. On receiving a "Red warning", Dad would immediately leave the house wearing his steel helmet and proceed to the village. Here he would blow his whistle throughout its length.

Looking at a map of Britain one might think that the Luftwaffe, the German air force, was hardly likely to expend much effort on this sparsely populated corner. It was very active however in laying mines by parachute, not always accurately, in the entrance of the strategically important Milford Haven. In 1940 and 1941 Red warnings and enemy aircraft overhead were by no means uncommon.

On one such occasion there was a real Dad's Army moment when my father, setting off to sound the alarm in the village at 2 a.m. approached the Fold in Marloes. It was a starry night and for once there were no searchlights to indicate anything untoward as he hurried along the edge of the field that lay between the lane from the School House and the Fold. Suddenly he was startled by a figure which sprang out from the darkness of the hedge. The vigilant Home Guard obviously thought that anyone out at this time of night must be at least a suspicious character and raised his weapon, a wooden club as he challenged my father. Fortunately my father was able to reassure him that they were both on the same side before any harm was done.

Having blown his whistle along the length of the village, he would return to the School House - much to my mother's relief. He would then await the next call indicating the end of the threat and return to Marloes to sound the "all clear". Warning of a gas attack would have been given by the sounding of a wooden rattle.

*In these politically correct days, younger generations have little idea of just how badly things were going for the Allies - Britain, the Commonwealth and France in the first year of the war. By May 1940 things were looking very serious indeed, most of northern France as well as Holland and Belgium having been overrun by the German army. The British Army had been driven back to the Channel coast and had concentrated in Dunkirk. In operation "Dynamo", 130,000 British troops and nearly 30,000 French troops were evacuated from the 9 mile stretch of sands around Dunkirk by the Royal Navy and an armada of little ships including small fishing boats and private yachts. These returned to the beaches time and again, in spite of heavy air bombardment from the Luftwaffe, to evacuate more fighting men to take them to England. Later in the summer furious air battles were fought over the English Channel, and the Kent and Sussex coast between R.A.F. Spitfires and Hurricanes and German Messerschmit fighters in what later became known as the Battle of Britain.*

In the School Log on 13 May 1940 my father recorded "Whitsun holiday restricted to 1 day owing to uncertainty of normal activities in war time". Soon after the start of the new term on 6 September 1940, my father wrote in the school log that "As all the other schools were closed due to lack of air raid shelters, I felt quite justified in taking the children down to picnic on the beach every afternoon since Wednesday. Fine weather with lots of swimming. Best of them to have certificates". I missed out on this because I had just started at Milford Haven County School. That wasn't the only extra curricular activity in Marloes that term and Hitler was not going to interfere with one of Dad's continuing missions in life - to give the children the opportunity to hear and appreciate the pleasures of "good music" whenever and wherever he could. In October he wrote in the School Log, "I took 15 seniors to a concert in St Ishmaels by the Dorian Trio. I had prepared some of the group, all the children enjoyed themselves".

It was about this time that the Pembrokeshire Education Authority announced that schools should not expect to open until 10 a.m. if there had been German air activity during the previous night. On 17 September, my father wrote "Air raid warning last night. Therefore school not opened until 10 a.m. I doubt the value of concession". Two weeks later on 1 October the log states "Air raid warning at 11.15 last night. In spite of this all children were at school at usual time. I opened at 9.30".

Enemy activity overhead was spasmodic over Marloes but I found the sweep of searchlights and the noise of anti aircraft fire always thrilling, never more so than the night when searchlights picked out a German aircraft which we could clearly see. He was bound to be shot down and I was going to see it happen. Unfortunately the raider escaped into cloud before the anti aircraft guns could do it any real harm. There were not infrequent air raid warnings but most of the damage in the area was caused by mines intended to be laid across the entrance to Milford Haven which had drifted on their parachutes to explode on land.

For me the first indication of the gravity of war came in August 1940 when I was happily riding on a farm cart "helping" with the corn harvest at Marloes Court. We were on our way to the far end of a field to gather another load of corn for threshing on a warm sunny afternoon. Black smoke in the east rapidly soon became a cloud rising into a clear blue sky. Very shortly we could see bright orange flames leaping into the air as the fire quickly grew bigger. At first we thought something must have happened in Milford Haven and then realised that the oil depot at Pembroke Dock, about 9 miles (15kms) away had been bombed. Our assumptions proved correct and as Vernon Scott records in "Harm's Way", for the next fortnight the huge column of smoke, "a sombre and awe-inspiring spectacle", was visible for many miles around. 11 out of a total of 17 oil tanks were destroyed in spite of efforts from fire brigades from all over the country. In all 650 firemen were involved in attempts to extinguish the fire and 5 Cardiff firemen lost their lives. The fire burnt for 18 days and some authorities suggest that it was Britain's largest fire since the Great Fire of London.

There was another less obvious threat to safety in the form of sea mines being washed ashore on the beaches. In the school log for 5 March 1941 my father recorded "A terrific detonation shook the village last night. On enquiry I found it to be due to a mine washed ashore at Musselwick Mouth. Have warned the children against going to the beaches especially at or near high water." In April 1941 the Germans were increasing their mine laying efforts and the School Log on 2 May records "Badly affected week. Planes overhead every night. Some children sleepy". Four days later he wrote "German plane dropped 150 - 200 incendiary bombs on Fopston fields last night. Galespring people received a nasty shock and 2 little girls, Nesta Phillips and Maureen Llewellyn both absent from morning session".

It was just 3 weeks later on the 26 March that the cable laying vessel Faraday, 2900 tons, was en route from Falmouth to Milford Haven with a cargo of 3870 tons of submarine cable. She was bombed off St Anne's Head by German aircraft and set on fire. 16 of the crew lost their lives. She managed to reach sheltered waters near Hooper's Point, the south eastern extremity of Marloes Sands, where her hulk remained visible for some months afterwards.

Cousin Peter Davies reminded me the other day of how a few months later, we with our fathers walked down to Marloes Sands one hot August afternoon. We were really looking forward to cooling off in the sea as we hurried onto the beach only to find that there was indeed a mine floating a few yards offshore. We beat a reluctant retreat and the climb back up the path had never before been so urgent. Back at School House an improvised shower using a watering can filled from the water butt refreshed us.

By 1941 the threat of a gas attack was waning when my father wrote in the School Log "For the time being I am leaving the carrying of gas masks to school to the discretion of parents".

That year, in an effort to allow older boys to help with the harvest without losing schooling, the school holidays were staggered. The second part of the summer holiday was taken from the 14 September to the 6th October "to release as much labour as possible for the delayed harvest". I remember that a party of senior boys from Milford County School were accommodated in a barn loft at Marloes Court from where they went out to work on various farms in the area.

For my parents, in every other way happy enough living in Marloes, there was one snag. They were tiring of the lack of amenities - no running water let alone a supply of hot water, outside lavatory and so on. The School House in Dale on the other hand had a piped supply of water, a boiler, a bathroom and an indoor lavatory so when the headmaster's post in Dale became vacant my father applied for it. He was appointed headmaster in November 1941. Before leaving he organized a Christmas Concert on 23 December. It was so successful that the concert was repeated on 6 January 1942 and raised the not inconsiderable sum of £10 2 shillings (£10.10p in today's money), in modern purchasing power the equivalent of about £410, a big sum considering the hardship and spending power of the village at that time. The proceeds were shared between the School Manager's Fund and the Serving Men's fund.

On 24 February 1942 my father wrote rather wistfully in the school log: "It is with many regrets that I take leave of this school".

# DALE

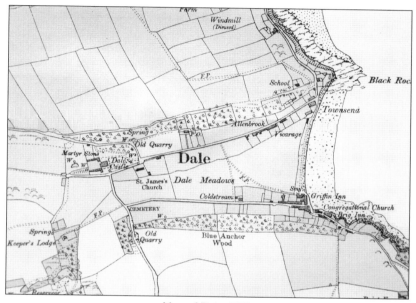

Map of Dale 1908

Just before we cross the parish boundary into Dale we pass Crabhall Farm on the left. In almost every way Crabhall farm is taken to be in Dale but it is in the parish of Marloes and part of the extensive Dale Castle Estate. In 1942 John and Annie Davies live here. Later Bunny Rind and his wife Beatrice ("Beata") follow them, having moved from St Ishmaels. In 1959 Peter James and his newly wedded wife, Ann take over the tenancy. After passing Crabhall Farm and still on the left, between the road and the sea, is a series of water filled gravel pits resulting from the wartime excavation of aggregate used for the building of the runways at the nearby aerodrome. Continuing on the road towards Dale, the first houses on the right are a pair of semi detached bungalows in one of which Audrey Howells lives and then come Jubilee Villas. Hughie and Stuart Fisher and their family live in one of these. A little further on the right is the lane to Upper and Lower Dale Hill Farms. "Lew" Williams farms the former which has lost some acreage in the building of the aerodrome. The Thomases are at

51

Lower Dale Hill and Howard Saies lives with his parents nearby. The road then passes the end of Pickleridge before climbing gently above the sea where there is a lane leading to the Davieses at Windmill Farm. The road twists and turns past Cliff Cottages before passing two bungalows which stand above the road on the right. In one of these the District Nurse, Nurse Powell lives.

Very soon we are at the top of the hill at Townsend. Edgar and Margaret Sturley live in the first house on the left, Hill Cottage. They have a son John, and daughter, Marjorie. John Green an evacuee from Chiswick lives very happily with them in a veritable home from home. Just below it on the right is the lane leading to the School, Canthill Cottage and School House.

Further down the hill is the start of the one way system, introduced early in the war to cope with the increased traffic in Dale and there is no entry into the road on the right. On this corner another branch of the Sturley family lives. Harold has joined the Navy leaving Frances, his wife and daughter Ann. Nearly 18 years later in 1960, Harold having survived the war, was taking a party of naturalists from the West Wales Field Society at Dale Fort to Skomer Island in his boat and killed when he had entered a live firing range. Tragically the requisite warning flags were not flying.

Dale from lane near Dale Point Farm

On the left is a footpath to Black Rock, enjoying an attractive situation overlooking the Haven and the Gan estuary. Still on the left and just beyond the path, the sea wall starts. Opposite Harold and Frances Sturley and behind a high wall on the right is the substantial Brook House to which Mr and Mrs Say have retired having returned to their native Pembrokeshire after a working life spent tea planting in India. Their son, John and daughter Pamela, are both at boarding school. Next is a small cottage with a corrugated metal roof, the home of the Sheppard brothers, Laddie and Charlie, two of the "characters" of the village. They are the postmen.

Adjoining them is Brook Cottage, where Mr and Mrs Seymour Reynolds live with their 3 sons, Campbell, Martin and Frank and 4 daughters, Gwyneth, Marion, Frances and Roma. Seymour Reynolds is a boat builder and skilled craftsman, a highly respected figure in the village.

The road then runs along the top of the beach. On the right it soon passes the drive to Allenbrook and Dale Nurseries. Allenbrook is a large rambling house where Col Rind and his wife live. Col Rind is home from a career in the Indian Army and he is now proprietor of Dale Nurseries, an important employer in the area. The Colonel has a strictly military bearing, conducting himself as though he is officiating in the Sovereign's Parade at Sandhurst.

The Griffin Inn and the Brig Quay

At the far end of the beach the sea wall is restored and the road squeezes round a sharp corner to pass between the wall and the Griffin Inn. On summer evenings, servicemen drink their beer standing at the sea wall because the small bar is packed. Next to it is another 3 storey building, Richmond House where an ornithologist and writer, R.M. Lockley lived for a short time. Later the Fry family (members it was said of the chocolate family) spent part of the war here. Adjoining this house is Eaton Hall used for a short time in the war as a Medical Reception Centre, a sort of cottage hospital, for the forces. At the end of Eaton Hall the road turns right into South St and on the opposite corner is another substantial house where Percy and Gertie Richards and their daughter Margaret live. They are members of the family of farmers who work Windmill Park in St Brides and Winterton and Fopston farms in Marloes. Percy Richards has an artificial leg resulting from a First World War injury.

Before we turn right into South St we continue a little further ahead and on the left is the path to the Quay. In the early 40's, the first house is a ruined shell and the third building is the Congregational Chapel. The large Edwards family live in the 4th house, the Brig which many years ago had been a pub, hence its slipway. I remember particularly Beryl, Gwyn and Joan; the other members of the family are somewhat older than me. Behind and above those buildings is Back St with a couple of cottages in one of which Gordon, Mona, Kenneth and Joy of the Phillips family live. The pretty lane continues past the entrance to Jack and Beatrice Davies at Point Farm to end at Dale Fort on the Point but in 1942 this is a restricted area.

Back at the end of South St, and running in a westerly direction, is Mrs Roch's shop on the left. She is assisted by her daughter Marjorie and her son in law, Gwyn Jenkins. As far as I recall there are no more houses on this side of South St in the area now known as Woodside and Blue Anchor Way. On the right almost opposite the shop is Eaton Lodge and next to it the Reading Room. More cottages on the right and then we are at Mrs Sturley's Post office. After this is the wooden Village Hall, the relic of a Field Hospital which had been set up in Dale Meadow in the 1914-18 war. The last house in the village proper is Coldstream House, a substantial house where brothers John and Billy Roch live with their parents. On the left, Blue Anchor Wood overlooks the whole length of the road which reaches a T junction and beyond the junction is the cemetery with its impressive marble War Memorial.

Here we'll take a left turn up a steepish hill curiously called the Drift. The road takes us past the lanes leading to Hayguard Hay, the Warlows at Broomhill, the Youngs at Maryborough and the Allens at Brunt farms. The last got its name from no less a person than Henry Tudor, on his way in 1485 to do battle with Richard III in the Battle of Bosworth Field. 15 days later, after victory at Bosworth, he would claim the Crown of England. He had apparently described his climb from his landing place in Mill Bay as "a brunt".

This road after passing the entrance to the radar establishment at Kete ends at windswept St Anne's Head with its lighthouse, foghorn and coastguard station. With family quarters for lighthouse keepers and coastguards it is a community in its own right especially as it is otherwise out of bounds except to military personnel manning the gun emplacements which guard the entrance to Milford Haven.

Retracing our steps to the T junction the Cemetery is now on the left and continuing straight ahead, the road turns sharply to the right as it passes below the boundary wall of Dale Castle, inhabited by generations of the

Lloyd - Philippses. Records reveal an original fortification of some antiquity but the present building is the result of a substantial makeover in the years before the First World War. Soon we are at the gate on the right leading down to the Parish Church of St James, a compact building with a much more attractive interior than its slightly ill proportioned tower suggests. Just beyond the church is the entrance to the walled garden of Dale Castle.

Dale Castle

Now, proceeding more or less eastwards towards the Haven, we are in what will later be known as Castle Way. We soon pass on the left the only house on this road for some distance, known in the 40s as the Old Post Office where the Gould family live. Behind it lies Castle Wood, the scene of many an escapade. On the right are Dale Meadow and then Dale Nursery and associated cottages; Nurse (Gladys) Bottin lives in one of them. Then we pass the long rear elevation of Allenbrook. A little further on the left, is the Women's Institute Hut and next, above the road stands the School House with its sloping garden and its neighbour, Canthill Cottage. Opposite the School House is the substantial Vicarage. In 1942 it is occupied by a large family of evacuees who have achieved some notoriety after chopping down a handsome mahogany banister for firewood. We are soon back on the road that we came in on, with a good view of Dale Roads and Milford Haven.

The civilian population of Dale in 1942 is about 250, the electoral register in 1935 containing 170 names.

.  .  .  .  .  .  .  .  .  .  .  .  .

The School House in Dale had modern plumbing and a piped water supply which, with an efficient boiler, meant the untold luxury of a real bath and for my mother relief from the drudgery of having to heat water to wash clothes. It also had a proper kitchen. There were no more trips to an outside lavatory but there was still no electricity or gas. Whereas the School House in Marloes was exposed to all points of the compass, at Dale it enjoyed a sheltered situation. With its elevated south facing position it overlooked much of the village, the beach and the Haven of Milford. From my bedroom window I could see the Martello Fort on Stack Rock, which had provided the setting for a cracking good adventure story, "Mystery in Milford Haven" by "Taffrail" which I had enjoyed a year or two earlier.

The School House

The beach, an expanse of mud at low spring tide, provided safe and pleasant swimming near high tide and was less than 5 minutes' away. There were boys of my own age, who had not been taught by my father, to get to know and sometimes get into mischief with. I remember particularly Frank Reynolds from Brook Cottage, John Roch from Coldstream, Hughie Fisher from Jubilee Villas and an evacuee, John Green who lived so happily with the Sturleys at Hill Cottage. A little later Howard Saies appeared on the scene when his parents moved from Dale Hill to a house near Allenbrook.

Milford Haven with its fine natural harbour was one of a number of West coast ports in which freighters and tankers assembled before joining an escorted crossing in convoy to the U.S.A. and Canada. 20 or more ships would congregate over 3 or 4 days before joining similar groups to make the hazardous Atlantic crossing where they were at risk from the torpedoes of German submarines and the guns of warships. The sight of these ships, the to and fro activity of minesweepers and patrol boats, the sound of gunfire as each departing ship fired a practice salvo as it left the safety of the Haven, all stirred the imagination of a 12 year old. After their departure the harbour might be almost free of shipping for a day or so but soon another convoy would assemble.

In the air Wellington bombers of R.A.F. Coastal Command flew low overhead if the wind was in a certain direction as they left for reconnaissance patrols over the Western Approaches in search of enemy U boats and shipping. In a few hours they would return. Over the Haven RAF Sunderland flying boats lumbered away from their base at Pembroke Dock as they slowly gained altitude. Their patrols were much longer. All this activity in the air and at sea was certainly exciting too.

In Dale in 1942 there were uniforms everywhere, gunners from the Blockhouse at St Anne's Head and anti aircraft installations, RAF types and WAAF's from the recently completed aerodrome. Later they were followed by sailors and WRENs when the Fleet Air Arm succeeded the RAF in the establishment known as H.M.S.Goldcrest.

The influx of service personnel resulted in much additional trade for the Griffin Inn. On summer evenings on the sea wall opposite the pub airmen, soldiers and later sailors would gather. There was a mild culture shock when WAAFs first appeared at the Griffin. We had not yet reached the times when nice girls went to pubs.

. . . . . . . . . . . .

From time to time we had interesting next door neighbours in Canthill Cottage which had been rented by the Forces for married quarters. The first neighbours that I can remember were the family of a Royal Artillery Captain stationed at the Block House on St Anne's Head. He was the son of a very famous publishing family, still a household name today. He had rented Canthill for his wife and son, B. B's parents were perfect neighbours, sociable and although well to do, without a trace of snobbishness, or as we used to say, "Side". B however, who was a couple of years younger than me, was to put it mildly a spoilt brat. He had a collection of trains, aeroplanes and cars that boys like me would only see in a Hamley's catalogue. The only reason that I ever spent time with him was so that I could play with his toys - a case perhaps of toy cupboard love.

On one occasion his natural peevishness and ill humour was aggravated, if such a thing were possible, when he developed measles. I was aware in the background of an elderly man of somewhat disreputable appearance who wore a navy blue cable knitted polar necked sweater and clearly down on his luck. He had just arrived to spend a few days with his friends, B's parents. What possible connection could such a seedy figure have with such an obviously prosperous family? As I was leaving, having borne B's unpleasantness for as long as I could, the scruffy visitor tried to press a half crown piece - 2/6 (12½ p) into my hand. Such an amount was serious money which I thought was perhaps a reward for my stoic tolerance of B's behaviour. The problem was - this old boy was obviously on his beam's end. There was only one thing I could do - refuse politely.

I told my parents about my afternoon and the half a crown that I had been offered by the scruffy old man and how I had refused it because he was so poor. My parents perhaps exchanged glances on hearing this because they might already have had an inkling of who the scruff was. Apparently B's parents and their guest, Lord Winster for that was who the shabby man was, were highly amused when they heard the full story.

My father in the school log tells us on 12 May 1942 that "I invited Lord Winster, until recently Commander Fletcher, Labour Member of Parliament for Nuneaton, to visit the school . . . . As I thought it an excellent opportunity for the children to hear him speak. His address was received with all the attention and enthusiasm we would have expected." His signature is in the school log. 5 years later Lord Winster became Governor General of Cyprus.

. . . . . . . . . . . .

It wasn't just the Griffin that benefited from the influx of service personnel. The Sunday evening congregation at St James Church had for some time been augmented by servicemen and my father was soon installed as organist. In no time at all a few of the servicemen joined the choir which perhaps for the first time ever in Dale, consisted of tenors and basses to supplement our feeble and at times discordant efforts. My father could realise his ambition to raise a choir that could sing anthems for now there were singers who could read music and harmonise and replace our hesitant unison. Such was the harmonious sound which filled the small church on Sunday evenings that I quite enjoyed putting in my third attendance of the day. The high point of choral music in Dale, at any rate in my father's time was an Easter Anthem, I think by John Stainer. It became better known later in a less elaborate form as the hymn "The strife is o'er, the battle done".

The Vicar of Dale, H.J.M. Lewis had joined the Army and had been replaced by a curate in charge who bore the resounding name of Avery Cattanach. My clearest memory of him was in a nautical rather than a pastoral context for Mr Cattanach was the Scoutmaster of the Sea Scouts. Quite soon after I had enrolled we were involved in a minor incident although at the time it seemed a much more serious matter because of wartime restrictions on the use of civilian craft in the Haven after sunset.

Four of us under "Captain" Cattanach's excitable command were rowing a small boat across the mouth of the Gan estuary one late summer evening. The incoming tide grew stronger as the estuary narrowed and soon it was taking us quite briskly upstream. The sun would soon be setting so there was no time to be lost if we were to get back to Dale before the curfew. We rowed back against the tide but no matter how hard we pulled, to the increasing anxiety of our captain, we were slowly but surely being taken upstream. He was now getting very fraught and exhorted us to pull yet harder and faster. The increase in the stroke rate resulted in one of us "catching a crab", missing the water completely with his oar. Inevitably the crab catcher fell back off his thwart and with feet flailing the air he landed in the bottom of the boat. The hoots of laughter that followed this totally incapacitated us and now we were proceeding backwards up stream at quite a good rate. Fortunately as the tide slackened we managed to get back to reach the beach at Dale just as the first stars appeared in the evening sky. It was one of my most enjoyable experiences in Scouting. For the record I must say that in spite of his extreme agitation, Mr Cattanach maintained a priestly vocabulary throughout. He left Dale quite soon after this but I am sure that his departure was not in any way connected with this episode.

Avery Cattanach's curacy was followed by the arrival of a new vicar, Iorwerth Thomas who was also interested in youth work. He was a good sport known rather disrespectfully behind his back as "Iorrie". He was also interested in aircraft and soon established the Air Scouts. The weekly meetings were held in the W.I.Hut and we particularly enjoyed the exercise of aircraft recognition in which we were required to recognize friendly and hostile aircraft by their silhouettes drawn on half postcard sized cards. The card was held up rather like the flash cards used by some teachers to teach reading. We took to this task with more enthusiasm than we ever showed for Geography or Latin. By now the U.S.A. was fully involved in the war and there must have been 35 or 40 different designs to learn to recognise immediately. R.A.F. planes like Wellingtons, Spitfires, Hurricanes and Ansons, German Messerschmits 109s and 110s, Dorniers, Heinkels and Junkers. Then there were U.S.A.A.F. Baltimore, Maryland and Liberator bombers, Wildcat and Thunderbolt fighters, all grist to our mill.

The youth or at any rate the boys reciprocated Mr Thomas' interest in them for he had a comely wife, Iris, who  had a good mezzo voice. She could have been a Katherine Jenkins lookalike and I can see and hear her now singing Mendelssohn's "I waited for the Lord" at one evensong.

Music making went on at the School House after Sunday evening service. It was open house to anyone who could sing. The small lounge would be packed with a dozen or so mainly service people, Gunners from the batteries and searchlight installations, WAAFS and RAF types from Dale Aerodrome and later Fleet Air Arm pilots, WRENS and Marines from H.M.S.Goldcrest. One civilian I remember was James Huck a physicist and music buff who was in charge of the "hush hush" Naval establishment at Dale Fort which we later learnt was a degaussing station, decreasing the vulnerability of ships to the magnetic mines regularly laid by German aircraft across the entrance to the Haven.

My father was of course in his element at his beloved Challen and a quite surprising array of musical talent found its way to the School House. Apart from enthusiastic amateurs this group included professional musicians - Judy Pullen Baker, a WREN, had been a violist in the Sadler's Wells orchestra and a Gunner who had been a member of the chorus of Carl Rosa Opera. He made grotesque facial contortions as he sang German lieder and the faces he pulled so amused Robin, George and me that we were forced to retreat behind the sofa where we dissolved into fits of silent laughter. I don't think there was much in the way of refreshment at these gatherings of all ranks because of food rationing but one or two people would mysteriously produce a packet of tea or sugar to supplement our rations.

St James' Church Dale

.   .   .   .   .   .   .   .   .   .   .   .

The tranquil atmosphere of Evensong was disturbed one evening by the late arrival of a man bent over almost double and limping badly. Walking was a spectacular and endless struggle against gravity and to help him stay on his feet, he supported himself with a walking stick. With his free hand he held his stomach. His face revealed that he was in some pain and he obviously had some difficulty in breathing. This arresting picture was completed by dark glasses worn in spite of the fading evening light. He took his seat, not at the back as any latecomer might be expected to do, but in one of the two or three vacant pews at the front. Not many minutes had elapsed when, as the vicar was reading at the lectern, there was a loud groan followed by a cough and further commotion as the poor chap staggered out of church. I suppose somebody must have followed him out to render assistance.

Behind and above me in the choir Arthur Rosewall, a warm Mancunian Royal Marines sergeant with a fine baritone voice and a regular Sunday evening visitor to School House, leaned over. He had something he wanted to tell me urgently. He traced the outline of two figures on the palm of his hand. I couldn't quite understand what he was trying to convey but it was clearly important and couldn't wait. He leant over and whispered hoarsely "V.C." My heart must have swelled with pride because now we had a war hero in our midst.

Back at the usual gathering at the School House after church, all listened intently while Arthur described our hero's background. Joseph Groundspan had been bayoneted in fierce hand to hand fighting in France. His courage had earned him the highest award for bravery, the Victoria Cross. After being invalided out of the army he had fallen on hard times. Having presented himself at H.M.S. Goldcrest Petty Officers' Mess, the Marine Sergeants took pity on him and fed and accommodated him for a couple of weeks. Shortly after what might be quite accurately described as his church parade, Joseph Groundspan V.C. disappeared quite suddenly without saying farewell and leaving no forwarding address.

Several months later there was a small paragraph in the News Chronicle stating that Josef Grunschpan had been sentenced to 3 months imprisonment by a London Magistrates' Court for obtaining money by false pretences by posing in the Savoy Hotel as a disabled war hero. I can't help thinking Josef Grunschpan must have been our very own "V.C.", Joseph Groundspan.

. . . . . . . . . . . .

Early in 1942 my parents gave me what they thought would be good news. My mother was going to have a baby, expected in early June. I must confess that I was not overjoyed at this prospect. True enough I had yearned for companionship to relieve a sometimes solitary existence in the School House in Marloes but that was years ago and this was altogether different. I was now 11 and was able to see much more of my contemporaries in the village. My first thoughts were - "WHAT WOULD THE BOYS THINK? WHAT HAD MY PARENTS BEEN UP TO? I was more embarrassed than anything else.

Jennifer arrived on a fine Sunday morning on the 7th June 1942. She must have been unsettled in her early weeks, perhaps by the nightly sound of anti aircraft fire and the occasional explosion of a wayward mine landing on the ground. Cousin Peter Davies reminds me that soon my mother took her away to St Davids, where things were quieter, for a few weeks. I have no clear recollection of this although I do remember one night when there was a lot of anti aircraft fire and a loud explosion in the area of Point Farm from yet another badly aimed mine. My father was out and about patrolling the village as usual and my mother and Jennifer were "sheltering" in a cubby hole under the stairs. In spite of her protestations and entreaties I remained in bed where I was warm and comfortable. Apart from anything else there was no room in the cubby hole for one more. I had reasoned that in the highly unlikely event of there being severe damage, I would be far better off lying in bed on top of all the rubble.

Occasionally it was suggested that I take Jennifer out in her pram. Having to endure the inevitable teasing from "The Boys" was an unappealing prospect but one day, when she was about a year old, in an uncharacteristic attack of virtue I agreed to take her out.

I did not tell my parents, however, that I planned this as a towing operation with my bike acting as a tug, pulling the pram with a 10 foot rope. I knew that starting the tow from the end of the lane, just below the Sturleys at Hill Cottage was going to produce far too much momentum and the pram had no adjustable brake. In any case there was 2 way traffic on the upper part of the hill. I wheeled the pram now roped to the bicycle partly down the incline to within 3 or 4 yards of the start of the one way system, hoping all the time that none of "The Boys" would see me with my hands on the pram. I was able to mount the bike whilst holding the pram back and we set off on our downhill journey.

We were making good progress when a cat decided to run across the road in front of me. I had to brake to avoid running over the wretched creature but now I had another problem because here came Jennifer strapped in her bucking and swaying pram hurtling past me as she careered down the last 7 or 8 yards of the hill. Her rapid progress was slightly impeded by the handle of the pram which struck a glancing blow to the high wall on the right that surrounded Mr Say's "Brook House". Fortunately the pram had a low centre of gravity and although there was a temporary loss of stability it remained on its four wheels. I soon caught Jennifer up and was able to resume the tow. We then proceeded along the road at the top of the beach in a much more dignified fashion before making a safe return. There was no obvious evidence of our mishap - the pram having sustained many scratches and bumps in the course of its long career. I don't know if my parents got to hear about our adventure but I cannot remember being asked to take Jennifer out in the pram again. When she was able to walk however, I used to take her out occasionally if I thought that The Boys were not about.

Jennifer with our parents, Trefor and Lilian

It was about this time that I would have brought further dismay to my parents had they learnt of a short organ recital I gave before Sunday school one rainy afternoon. Sunday School was held in the church at 2.30 p.m. This day I set off allowing plenty of time for the usual quick "drag" on half a cigarette in the quiet lane which ran uphill along the wall of Dale Castle, the remainder to be enjoyed after Sunday School. Having met the usual miscreants and lit up, the threatened rain soon arrived in a downpour so we stubbed out our fags and sought refuge in the church where there now had gathered 4 or 5 other Sunday scholars. In spite of my attempts to keep it from them (after all it was only girls and "sissies" who played the piano) it was known that I could play a few tunes and I was prevailed upon to play my most recent party piece, a very silly song called Maresytoats, the words of which went:

> Maresy toats (Mares eat oats)
>
> And doesy toats (And does eat oats)
>
> Andlittle lambsy tivy, (And little lambs eat ivy)
>
> Akid'lly tivytoo (A kid will eat ivy too)
>
> Wouldn't you?

I was playing this on the organ and one or two of Dale's finest were singing along when who should appear, much earlier than expected, but the Vicar, Iorwerth Thomas. His expression was as dark as the sky outside and I was suspended for the day. Fortunately being a good sort "Iorrie" did not pass on details of my transgression to my parents.

. . . . . . . . . . . . . .

In 1941 a radar station at Kete was established. Radar had been discovered in 1935 so at that stage the technology was still evolving. Later it became a training centre for radar operators and direction officers as well as an important observation centre keeping a long range look out over sea and air. At first it was manned by the RAF but a couple of years later the Royal Navy took it over when it became known as HMS Harrier. Quite soon after we had moved to Dale we had billeted with us a young boffin in the person of a RAF Pilot Officer who was stationed at RAF Kete. He was not long out of University and very recently commissioned. Unfortunately he might have been a brilliant physicist but he lacked any semblance of personal skills. He clearly felt that this was a master servant situation, he of course the master. Things came to a head one night when in the manner of a haughty colonel addressing an incompetent batman, he ordered my father something. My father would do anything to further the war effort but this was too much. The Pilot Officer was gone in a day or two.

As boys in Dale in 1942 we were fully aware of the menace of spies. The path to West Dale beach lies in a valley above which the cliffs rise quite steeply to the North and South. To the North the land flattens out and this area was now the site of the fully operational aerodrome. To the South stood the radar station at Kete. It seemed obvious to us that either establishment would be a centre of attention for spies so in an attempt to help the War Effort we occasionally patrolled the coast around West Dale in search of enemy agents.

One evening as the light faded we spotted a deeply suspicious character who was peering out to sea and scanning the horizon, anxiously it appeared to us, as he paced back and for on the cliffs towards the airfield. Clearly he must be a spy who had completed his mission and was now waiting to be picked up by a U boat after dark. We therefore had to keep him under close observation. Unfortunately his field skills were better than ours for he gave us the slip as the light faded. This was a huge disappointment but we consoled ourselves that he was probably only a bird watcher after all.

In the course of our counter intelligence activities, on summer evenings on the cliffs to the South of West Dale beach we had started watching birds albeit of the unfeathered type, WAAFS at first and then WRENS, stationed at the aerodrome and Kete. They played a vital part in helping keep up the morale of the airmen and sailors stationed there. We had noticed from time to time WRENS and WAAFS, sailors and RAF types, ambling along the cliffs above West Dale and this too required further investigation.

There have been many land slips on the cliffs in this area resulting here and there in a grassy platform, perhaps 20 yards wide in places, and 10 to 15 feet below the cliff top which was our vantage point. From here our view of the stage below was as good as the front row of any dress circle. The platform was partly separated into compartments by mounds from minor land slips which afforded a certain degree of privacy. It was rather like a series of communicating rooms. Behind us the ground fell back quite quickly.

Occasionally in the course of our reconnaissance we would come across a couple whose desire for each other couldn't wait for the privacy of nightfall, or at least twilight, before getting down to the real business of the evening. On one balmy late spring evening we were carrying out surveillance operations on a sailor and a WREN a few yards away. Such was the intensity of the sailor's approaches it seemed unlikely that the lovers were going to be able to wait even for deep twilight. The sailor was fully dressed but the WREN'S lingerie was on display. As we observed the scene below in great anticipation of what must surely follow, another naval pair came round the corner below us and stopped by the objects of our attention. In coming up the field behind us they had completed a rear encircling movement and so intent had been our attention to the developments unfolding below us, we had not noticed them. Now the sailor was indicating to his shipmate as he pointed at us that the lovers had an audience. The passionate sailor shot to his feet - a reckless action you might think at this stage of the proceedings - and bounded up the bank towards us in hot pursuit. It was time to make a quick exit and laughing and running down the sloping field, we stumbled into a crescent of gorse bushes. Here we had the second surprise of the evening. Inside the crescent of gorse and enjoying almost total privacy until this very moment, we nearly ran over the partly undressed sister of one of our number (an evacuee since you ask) and her lover who hadn't waited for nightfall.

. . . . . . . . . . . .

The entrance to the haven was guarded by an artillery battery stationed at West Blockhouse Point. With East Blockhouse near Angle on the other side of the water it dominated the Haven entrance at its narrowest point, just over 1.5 miles across. Dale Fort a further mile inside the harbour at Dale Point was the location of an establishment staffed mainly by civilians and housed a "Degaussing" system which decreased the vulnerability of ships to magnetic mines which were regularly laid across the Haven entrance by German aircraft.

Occasionally ill directed German mines dropped by parachute and intended to be laid across the Haven entrance used to land in the area causing loud explosions and blast waves. As far as I know there were no casualties in the Dale area. If the respective school logs are anything to go by there were more incidents in Marloes up to February 1942 than there were in Dale from then on, presumably reflecting the progress of the war. On the other hand the Luftwaffe continued its bombing of the cities with unrelenting ferocity throughout 1943 and 1944.

The military population in the area was briefly increased in 1943 by the arrival of some U.S. soldiers who camped for a few days on the broad verge of the road as it passed above Dale beach. They stayed there for just a few days. The shortness of their stay was a little disappointing as they were extremely generous handing out chewing gum and sweets, both items in short supply because of rationing. As occasional smokers we were also delighted when they gave us Lucky Strike and Philip Morris cigarettes although we were now connoisseurs who preferred Woodbines or Players. We never knew why they were there - it was some time before the Normandy invasion. In wartime one learnt not to ask questions because there would be no answers. "Careless Talk Cost Lives" were the words on posters everywhere.

Later some landing craft, (LCT s), with their flat bottoms and shallow drafts sailed right on to the beach. On grounding the ramp was lowered and jeeps drove down the ramp and up the beach but I have no recollection of any large scale disembarkation. It was also quite exciting to watch the arrival on a couple of occasions of a number of amphibious vehicles called Ducks (actually DUKWS) coming ashore on Dale beach.

It was in April 1943 that an incident off St Anne's Head resulted in one of the biggest losses of life in the war not directly due to enemy action. Although there was no mention of it on the radio or in the papers, the true extent of the disaster began to leak out gradually. In Dale there was much collective grief especially when rumours circulated that human error in the shape of officialdom was responsible. It was some years afterwards that the truth was known.

*A convoy of experimental landing craft had set out from Belfast where they had been modified as Landing Craft Guns (LCG's). LCG 15 and LCG 16 were in passage to Falmouth from where they would sail to the Mediterranean in preparation for the forthcoming beach landings in Sicily. Unfortunately modifications had not been completed before leaving Belfast. Having taken on supplies at Holyhead they continued their voyage along the west coast of Wales. During their passage, LCG 15 and LCG 16 got into difficulties as the weather deteriorated quite unexpectedly with high winds followed by a severe gale. In the rough seas both LCGs started shipping water. They sought permission to shelter in Fishguard Harbour but were refused entry. Thence they set out for Milford Haven, and by the time they arrived in this area the weather had deteriorated further. Here the anti submarine boom was closed and the authorities, fearing that a German submarine might enter the Haven as well, refused to open it.*

*A couple of hours later LCG 15 sank. People from the other side of the Haven watched in horror as they saw the crew and 30 marines dashed against the cliffs below. Worse was to follow.*

*HMS Rosemary, an escort ship in the area, had been diverted to assist and now attempted to get a tow line to LCG16. After several attempts failed, 6 men in Rosemary's whaler volunteered to take a towline to the LCG but the small boat was soon swamped and all aboard the whaler were lost. Here the fates dealt a further blow. The Angle Lifeboat was off station for periodic overhaul and because of wartime difficulties there had been no substitute. The nearest lifeboat at St David's was called to assist but had to battle its way through high seas and heavy weather and did not arrive in the area until 1 a.m. Sadly LCG16 had foundered an hour earlier. Eventually the lifeboat found just one survivor who was taken back to St Davids and then to hospital. Also in the hospital were just two other survivors who had been washed ashore from LCG15. 84 lives were lost in this disaster. The coxswain of the St David's Lifeboat William Watts Williams, a cousin of my mother, was awarded the RNLI medal for his bravery and seamanship on this occasion.*

. . . . . . . . . . . .

A few months later, we were somewhat surprised one day to see in the bay half a ship, the stern section of the tanker Athel Duchess, which was to be a familiar sight for the next few years.

*In August 1943 the 9000 ton tanker had just left Milford Haven in convoy and was forced out of line and grounded on The Smalls. Two tugs attempted to tow her off at the next high tide but she could not be moved. The remaining 56 crew were taken off by the St David's lifeboat. Later she broke her back and the bow section soon sank. The stern section was salvaged and towed into Dale Roads where she spent the next four years.During that time, the stern section was manned by one Officer, an Officer`s steward, and the Chief Engineer.*

*Eventually she was bought by Norwegians and fitted with a new bow section and returned to sea in 1948 as the Milford. Thereafter she sailed under 6 different owners and at least once was lengthened to become a dry cargo bulk carrier. Her sea going days ended in 1954 when she became an oil depot ship in the port of Antwerp.*

Athel Duchess lying off Dale in 1944, taken with box camera.

The Chief engineer John Rosine, a Scot was to find romance as a result of this mishap on one of his visits ashore. He met and married Barbara Edwards, one of the Edwards family who lived in the Brig, in Dec 1943.

. . . . . . . . . . . . .

The move to Dale had caused no disruption in my schooling because by now, February 1942, I was in my 6th term at Milford. There was one downside, however, and that was the extra 20 minutes in each direction for the bus journey to school. This meant catching the bus at 7.45 a.m. and returning at 5.15 p.m. at the earliest and after tea an hour or more of homework. The journey to school passed quickly enough - perhaps there was some vocabulary to go over or last minute revision before a test or terminal exam.

While Haverfordwest boasted a Headmaster's Conference School, Haverfordwest Grammar school and a girl's school - Tasker's, Milford Haven County School was a co educational local authority secondary school, entry to which required passing the "Scholarship" exam (later known as the 11 plus.) The County School soon became a Grammar School and survived as the last Grammar School in Wales against all the odds until 1988.

In the 1930's, apart from Tom Martin and Jack Rayner who went to Haverfordwest Grammar School and Pamela MacTaggart who went to Tasker's, only a very few pupils from the area went on to secondary education. Although Milford Haven County School did not produce many candidates for Oxbridge, standards in academic subjects and sports were high. In 1940 there were about 300 pupils divided among 3 Houses named, as befits a port, after seafarers: Greville, Nelson and Starbuck. The first two were famous Admirals who at some time in their career had a connection with the port. The third named, Starbuck recognized the contribution that an eponymous Quaker family from Nantucket Island, Massachusetts made to the development of Milford as a fishing port in the early 1800s. Later as the school expanded a fourth house was created. Hamilton was named after another Admiral whose wife became much better known than her husband.

The Headmaster, R.R.Finney was a Lancastrian and behind his fierce demeanour lay a genial disposition. Nevertheless he could cause knees to tremble when circumstances required but he rarely found it necessary to resort to the cane. "You blithering idiot" was his favourite and gloriously politically incorrect form of rebuke.

In spite of the war which had resulted in some of the masters being called up, high standards of teaching and discipline were maintained. Virtually every master and mistress were honours graduates who wore gowns at all times. On Speech Days (held in the Astoria Cinema), the staff wore hoods as well as mortar boards and on one memorable occasion, the great actress Sybil Thorndike (later Dame Sybil) presented the prizes. She was performing in a production of Euripides' Medea for forces and civilians in the area under the auspices of the Entertainments National Service Association, better known as "ENSA". Some wag however had suggested that it really stood for "Every Night Something Awful". It's difficult to see how a Greek tragedy would be used to stiffen morale today.

The school day started at 9 a.m. with Assembly in the hall which, with its wall bars, beams hoisted to the ceiling and climbing ropes tied back, doubled as a gymnasium. On the stage, the staff in their gowns stood behind Mr Finney who conducted a short act of worship which included the Lord's Prayer and a hymn. This was followed by results of school matches, house matches and mention would be made if someone like Bobby Limbrick or Monty Minter had scored a hatrick as both at different times were prone to do. An announcement would be made if there was a special event like a visiting speaker or perhaps a concert.

One speaker, an Army Chaplain was the brother of General (later Field Marshal) Bernard Montgomery better known as "Monty of El Alamein" and already famous. He recalled that he had served with the vicar of St Catherine's in Milford Haven, Rev. Haydn Parry in the North African campaign. Apparently the Vicar had served with distinction and had been awarded a M.C.

From time to time at Assembly, there would be news of an old boy who had been killed or reported missing. Less frequently the news would bring some relief when someone previously reported missing was now known to be a Prisoner of War. Of the 300 or so former pupils who had joined up 21 lost their lives. Two old boys were decorated posthumously, one receiving the D.F.C. and the other the D.F.M.

One day shortly after the war had ended, Mr Finney had a particularly sad announcement to make at Assembly. David Rice of 3A had died. It was all the more tragic because he was the long awaited only child of that good man, Dr Rice our family doctor. 13 year old David was a couple of years younger than me but I remember him as a chubby cheerful chap. It created as deep an impression on me as the death of the only survivor of the shipwrecked trawler, "Sea Breeze" nearly 10 years earlier.

On a lighter note there might be an announcement that the Dorian Trio would be giving a concert of chamber music. For those of us living in the country and acquainted with the night time arrangements for a pee, this would cause a few sniggers but these were nothing compared with the reaction of the younger boys in the audience later when the elderly lady cellist placed her instrument between her knees. It might have been that very lady cellist that the famous conductor Sir Thomas Beecham referred to when he was heard to say, "Madam you have a thing of great beauty between your legs but all you do is sit there and scratch it".

The dinner break came at 12.30 and lasted until 2 p.m to accommodate two sittings for school dinner. I'm sure the cooks did their best with the materials and equipment available in difficult times but the food was often poor and sometimes dreadful. It was much worse fare than any I encountered as a private soldier doing National Service. Breakfast had been at 7.30 a.m. and it's surprising what young digestive systems cope with 5 hours later with only a milk drink in the meantime.

From time to time we had stewed whale meat which had the colour and texture of beef casserole, a fish called called snoek and a particularly unpleasant form of powdered potato called Pom. The unwholesomeness of the first course was  sometimes relieved by the puddings which were usually much appreciated - particularly bread and butter pudding, treacle tart and jam roly poly. But there could be disappointments too and the frog spawn-like tapioca I still recall with revulsion.

The school day finished at 4 p.m. In the early years there would be about at least an hour's homework each night, the subjects being rotated through the course of a week. One form of punishment was detention for ½ an hour after school but as a country pupil with no means of getting home after the School bus had left, I escaped this imposition although I did not escape retribution. Instead I was given 100 or more lines. If this happened it was difficult to conceal this from vigilant parents who wondered why homework was taking longer than usual.

The homeward bus journey was much longer than the journey to school. Unlike the Saturday service bus to Haverfordwest, the school bus with its wooden seats was mechanically quite reliable. Invariably it was waiting outside the school when we came out and left at 4.15 p.m. Boarding the bus as one passed by the driver, one noticed the strong and unmistakable smell of stale beer, his bloodshot eyes and bleary look. Apart from the occasional playful scuffle the roundabout homeward journey, making a loop around St Ishmaels, was usually uneventful but it became tiresome when we arrived at Mullock Bridge where the driver lived. By now tummies would be rumbling furiously particularly if, as was so often the case, school dinner had not been up to scratch.

At Mullock Bridge the driver parked the bus on the road below the Police House. Without a word he would leave us to our own devices for up to 15 minutes whilst he went to his house 40 yards up the Dale road for a cup of tea and presumably a comfort stop. It says a lot for the forbearance of his passengers, and for that matter their parents, that there was little in the way of protest. The latest I remember getting back to Dale was 5.45 p.m., making a 10 hour school day before a start was made on homework. The circuitous 13 mile journey had taken 1½ hours. We were a pretty hungry pack by the time we got home even though we had usually attempted to stave off our hunger by clubbing together to buy a loaf of bread tearing it into roughly equal portions to divide among the 5 or 6 contributors.

. . . . . . . . . . . .

B.H. John was the History master who sometimes also took Art. He was a delightful man who, no longer having a wife was a sort of Mr Chips figure. He found it difficult to keep order in the classroom. It was rumoured that he had a metal plate in his skull following a First World War head injury. One might think that armed with this graphic knowledge we might have been more sympathetic with this good natured man but not a bit of it.

I remember three mistresses particularly who were all first class teachers. They were the diminutive Bessie Williams who taught Maths and was also the "Senior Mistress", the equally diminutive but hugely busted Sian Pugh who taught French and Mabel Jones who taught Latin. Miss Jones wore a grim expression and a hairstyle consisting of plaited hair tightly coiled over both ears rather like modern ear protectors.

A woodwork master whose name I can't now recall was a high profile figure for not altogether the right reasons for he was a practised player of "Pocket Billiards". Very occasionally, and I imagine reluctantly, a girl would have to enter his all male domain - the woodwork room which as a wooden building stood apart from the main school - perhaps with a message. Such an event would be carefully followed by the whole class because we knew that after his initial and thorough head to toe appraisal, a leer would follow and even as the girl retreated, gentle massaging could then be observed. As far as I know that happily was the limit of his aberration.

The most colourful of all the 15 or so staff was D.W. Walters, who taught English. He was a small man of slight build who strode the corridors with great purpose. His most arresting feature was a facial deformity, with a lower jaw seriously out of alignment and one eyelid drooped to half closure. His teeth would have given an orthodontist employment for months. Swept back wavy hair and a pair of thick horn rimmed glasses completed a somewhat sinister picture. Perhaps his disfigurement was the result of a birth injury although darker reasons were sometimes suggested. In spite of his unattractive appearance he enjoyed a certain reputation as a bit of a ladies' man. As well as teaching English he had a passion for amateur dramatics and as producer extracted polished performances from the local dramatic society, the Garrick Players in light plays like Dodie Smith's "I Captured the Castle", Barrie's "Quality Street" and Esther McCracken's "Quiet Weekend".

He was a brilliant teacher who kept the class on its toes. He had written at least two textbooks on English Grammar which needless to say were used in Milford. With a certain flamboyance he would sweep into the form room, clasp and then rub his hands together saying "Well what shall we talk about today?" or "Ask me anything you like". He had long ago drummed into us the dry elements of syntax; now he wanted us to widen our horizons.

These digressions were particularly frequent, of all times, in the year we were due to take the School Certificate of the Central Welsh Board ("The C.W.B."). To succeed candidates had to attain 5 passes at the same time. There were 3 grades of Pass - "Distinction", Credit", and "Pass" and of course "Fail". If Credits were obtained in English, English Literature, Mathematics, Latin and a modern foreign language (French usually), a further qualification known as Matriculation was awarded.

Our set books in School Certificate English were Macbeth, Sheridan's "The Rivals", substantial parts of Palgrave's Golden Treasury and Siegfied Sassoon's "Memoirs of a Fox Hunting Man". Incidentally David Thomas, the brother in law of D.H.Lloyd the former vicar of St Brides and Marloes, who was killed in the Somme was mentioned in this book.

What with Caesar's Gallic Wars Book V and Vergil's Aeneid as set books in Latin, French, Chemistry and History as well as Mathematics all to be passed with Credit simultaneously, we felt that we had plenty on our plates without D.W. Walters' efforts to develop our minds at this particular stage of our schooling. Some of his discourses and debates would last the full 40 minutes of the period. The inevitable result was that by the start of the summer term we were well behind in the syllabus. D.W.'s solution was to bring us in on three Saturday mornings at 9.30 a.m. for a 2 hour catch up session. This was no great problem for those who lived near but the only bus service from Dale was the school bus which ran Mondays to Fridays.

Those of us who lived in faraway Marloes and Dale had a choice between either a 10 mile cycle ride in each direction at 7.30 a.m. for a 9.30 a.m. start, or miss some important teaching. Secretly I quite enjoyed these trips because I was out of parental supervision on a thoroughly virtuous cause. I had an alibi and it provided a frisson of excitement and a rare opportunity to have a cigarette and a lemonade at a slightly shady café, Rabbaiotti's with urban friends before making my way home. I cannot recall a single word of complaint from either pupil or parent about these Saturday sessions. How different today.

. . . . . . . . . . . .

The war saw the call up of some masters to the Forces. Two of them I didn't see until after the war was over. David Roberts was the handsome Biology master who, in the RNVR, spent much of his sea time as a First Lieutenant on a destroyer escorting North Atlantic convoys whilst Trevor Lewis had been in the Royal Marine Commandos.

Some of their female replacements were really quite attractive, giving D.W. Walters further food for thought and perhaps provoking further flights of fantasy in the woodwork master. One lady Biology teacher was particularly striking. She had all the attributes which would have earned her a Hollywood screen test. She was however, neither a disciplinarian nor had much idea of how to hold a class' attention apart, that is, from just standing there exhibiting her tall, curvy figure. During one practical lesson in the biology lab I incurred her displeasure not once but twice. Firstly I had impersonated Adolf Hitler by holding a model of a small fish under my nose as a moustache and raising my left arm in the Nazi salute which had amused one or two of my neighbours. Later, as she walked round the bench where I was sitting, I accidentally knocked the aforesaid fish off the bench to the floor. She must have thought I had some dark ulterior motive, and presumably thinking that the fish on the floor was no coincidence, she sent me out of the lab for the rest of the period.

Being sent out of the room was always a potentially dangerous situation as it was just one step short of being sent to the Headmaster who occasionally toured the corridors in the course of his duties. If he saw you standing outside, an explanation would be sought. It was about 10 minutes before the end of the lesson and as I had been sent to Mr Finney earlier in the week for a previous indiscretion and already had one dressing down as a "blithering idiot", I was most anxious not to meet him again quite so soon. I therefore made a quick escape to the lavatory where I hid until the bell signalled the end of the lesson. This was strictly against the rules and in my anxiety to get back to stand by the door of the biology lab before

73

Miss Hollywood left the room, I made the mistake of leaving the lavatory even as the bell started to ring. I was immediately spotted by a busy body master who then marched me to the Headmaster's study. I was to have my second face to face meeting with Mr Finney within the week.

. . . . . . . . . . . .

Smoking in Milford had now become a habit for me. In breaks and after yet another ghastly school dinner, smokers gathered in an area behind the air raid shelter known as "Dragger's Union". On a calm day a thick blue grey pall hung in the air. The problem was how to finance the habit because pocket money like the family budget was tight.

The difficulty was solved after I had bought a cigarette from one of my more prosperous classmates for two pence (a fraction under 1p in modern money). A packet of 10 Players cigarettes in the war cost 1s 2d, (14 pence and 6p in today's currency). One didn't need to be a mathematician to realise that if I could sell 7 cigarettes at two pence each, the remaining 3 for my personal consumption would cost me nothing. In due course I was able to amass enough capital to pay for my initial investment - my first packet of 10. I soon had a loyal clientele although I never allowed credit and this financed my 1 or 2 a day habit for the rest of my schooldays.

One of the big drawbacks of living in Dale whilst attending Milford was the lack of opportunity to participate in out of hours activities especially sports - not that I had any great ability in either cricket or soccer. As it was I just made the team as a wing half for my House, Starbuck, but that was the limit of my achievement.

Later on I played in the first game of rugby ever played in Milford. This was initiated shortly after the arrival of John Hayes a new Latin Master from the Llanelli area. A few of us including two comedians, Kenneth ("The Stoat") Russell and "Sam" Sturley expressed interest and on a bone hard pitch and using the soccer posts as goal posts a match was played between two scratch sides. As I was one of a very few who knew the basic principles of the game and some of the laws, I played at scrum half, not a good place to be when most of the players knew nothing about offside laws. It was at the end of the Easter term in 1947, and although the ground was frozen hard no serious injuries resulted although a few of us had several friction grazes from the hard ground.

. . . . . . . . . . . .

My father had deeply embarrassed me when he was out first ball when playing cricket for Marloes against Dale. Now 8 years or so later I was playing for Dale against Marloes, this time on a field belonging to Point Farm. The ground was on a par with the Marloes ground with gentle slopes both length ways and crossways. Cows had recently grazed and had left their mark here too. It was a fine early summer evening and even though the School Certificate exams were approaching, I thought watching the Dale v Marloes match for a couple of hours, the maximum duration of a Dale v Marloes fixture, would be good relaxation and a chance to meet old acquaintances. The Dale team was one man short and there being no other spectators I had to make up the numbers. Marloes was batting first and to my dismay a snick was soon flying past my right hand. I lunged for it and in doing so my right shoulder collided with the hip of one of our better built players. I felt something "go" in my right shoulder and I fell to the ground in some pain.

This giant had obviously felt next to nothing of our collision but knew of the association between immobility of the shoulder after injury and frozen shoulder. Clearly he thought the effect of immobility was immediate because he bent over me as I lay on the ground and proceeded to move my arm through the full arc warning me that if I didn't start using it right away, it "will stiffen up, boy". Perhaps he had concluded that, because of my still frail physique, I was making a fuss about nothing. In spite of my protests, for what seemed ages but probably not more than 30 seconds, he continued to put my shoulder through a full range of movements.

I made my own way home, taking a short cut over the hedge rather than the longer way through the gate. Unfortunately the short cut necessitated a jump down of perhaps 2 feet on to the lane and another painful jolt. Today it would mean a trip to A&E at Withybush Hospital in Haverfordwest within the hour. As it was, I got back to the house about half a mile away unassisted. The next morning I went to see our neighbour in Canthill Cottage who at this time was a naval doctor, Surgeon Lieut. John Ryle. He arranged a strictly unofficial x ray at the sickbay of H.M.S. Goldcrest. The x ray unsurprisingly showed a broken collar bone and a collar and cuff and a sling were advised for the next three weeks.

The oral exam in French was just 4 weeks away and I thought I might be able to extract some advantage from this injury and the sling would be a good talking point. With the assistance of my French teacher Miss Pugh, who was not aware that the sling could be removed a week before the viva, I was well prepared with answers to any questions that the examiner might ask about my injury. In the meantime I hoped that I wouldn't meet Dr Ryle during this self-extended period of incapacity and went in to the viva quietly confident. In spite of leaning forward with my shoulder towards the examiner to emphasise my obvious injury, he totally ignored it. He was content merely to know where I lived, how far away I lived, how I got to school, what I'd had for breakfast that morning, what had I seen on my way to school that morning, what my interests were and all the other questions that French oral examiners used to ask.

. . . . . . . . . . . . .

Here I must quickly turn the clock back to my early days in Dale. I'm sorry to say that at the age of 12 and later I was still immature enough to enjoy teasing adults. In Dale there were two bachelor brothers who were natural targets for our pranks - Laddie and Charlie Sheppard. They both presented unusual appearances, Laddie usually sporting a dark stubble in spite of his duties as Postman. Charlie on the other hand was almost spruce but he was also the more unpredictable. He had metal framed glasses, a piercing stare and the long stride of a tallish man, leaning forward as though battling into the teeth of a Force 8 gale. Nevertheless he could cover the ground very quickly without appearing to be in a great hurry. This nearly caught us out once or twice.

Laddie and Charlie lived in a small cottage, which had a galvanised iron roof, next to Brook Cottage where Seymour Reynolds and his family lived. Frank avoided playing any part in our games with Laddie and Charlie not simply because they were his neighbours but because he was a kind soul. One of our games was to throw quite large stones, collected from the shore a few feet away, on to their metal roof. These would create a tremendous din and we would wait for one or the other, usually Charlie, to emerge from the doorway like a greyhound out of the trap and give chase, before we pedalled away on our bicycles.

After the war when fireworks were available again and we were old enough to know better, we used to set off an infernal firework known as a Jacky Jumper behind unsuspecting folk. Once ignited it would bang and jump in random fashion creating an illusion for the victim that it was following him. One day we managed to lure Charlie over to the sea wall opposite Eaton Hall and engage him in deep conversation as we sought his advice or opinion on some matter. It was not yet high water but the spring tide was well up the sea wall against which our bicycles rested.

When it was judged that Charlie was sufficiently involved in the conversation one of us, who shall be nameless, stood behind Charlie's back and lit the fuse. This was the signal for a general scattering and Charlie must have wondered what was going on but only for a second or two. The firework went off and poor Charlie nearly jumped out of his skin, much to everybody's merriment. Our laughter suddenly stopped however, as Charlie picked up the nearest bicycle and hurled it over the wall into 3 or 4 feet of sea water as if it was an empty cereal packet.

I'm afraid we spent a lot of time on our bikes endlessly pedalling through what were the ruins of the first house on Dale quay. There was other aimless activity too but the Reading Room came into its own on cold winter nights. Although it had no books or papers it had a billiard table. Many happy hours were spent there. It is said that being good at Billiards is a sign of a misspent youth. If this old saying is true I should be much better than I am at Billiards for you may well feel that much of my youth was misspent.

. . . . . . . . . . . .

The war in Europe ended in May 1945 and VE Day was celebrated as well as it could be given the shortage of many staples. The Griffin was well patronised but for many, celebration was muted. For some families there was continuing grief rather than joy. Gwyneth Thomas, the eldest daughter of the Reynolds family and Frank's sister, of Brook Cottage had lost her husband Herbert. His ship HMS Gould, a frigate, had been torpedoed in the Atlantic. He also left a son, Brian and a daughter, Angela whom he had not seen. James Lloyd was killed when his minesweeper was attacked by a German bomber. A Lieutenant in the Parachute Regiment married to one of the Richards family had been killed in the airborne assault at Arnhem.

I had not yet been able to add alcohol to my catalogue of vices, apart from the very occasional swig of home brewed cider, but  the previous autumn in anticipation of the great day we had buried a couple of flagons of what we thought was going to be a sloe based alcoholic drink. The method was simple. Into a flagon we put in about a 1/3 full of sloes, a little yeast and as much sugar as we could get our hands on and filled the bottle with water. The bottles were then buried in John Roch's garden and allowed to ferment and mature. I imagine that there was about as much alcohol in our concoction as there was phenol in Lewis' Drops years earlier but we must have been overcome by the euphoria of the occasion. Having had a mouthful or two of this not altogether unpleasant brew we found ourselves in the late evening sunshine whooping  past the  Post Office and going towards the seawall,  bending down and then straightening up trying to "hit" various targets with the shadows  cast by the top of our heads from the low sun. Such is the power of auto suggestion.

After the war my mother took in two P.G.s. (Paying Guests), Michael Ayrton and his wife Joan. Michael was the son of Barbara Gould a poet whose leftish views he had inherited and with which my father strongly agreed. He was a sculptor, painter and writer and in later years, an occasional broadcaster on Radio 4's "Any Questions". The Ayrtons had come to Pembrokeshire on the suggestion of Michael's mentor, the artist Graham Sutherland who was a regular visitor to the county, usually staying at Sandy Haven. My father used to have long discussions with Michael on music, art and politics. Michael knew the composer Constant Lambert quite well and on one matter my father and he were not in harmony, the value of Modern Music. I still have in its original dust jacket a copy of "Music Ho" subtitled "A Study of Music in Decline" by Constant Lambert, signed by Lambert and inscribed by Michael in a script with many flourishes "For Trefor - to shake him again - from Michael with affectionate greetings."

All this might suggest that I was becoming a bit of an intellectual but nothing could be further from the truth. At the age of 15 the things I liked best about Michael were his wife, Joan and his cigarettes. Michael smoked Passing Cloud - slightly longer than the standard brands and oval in cross section and very expensive. Here I have another confession to make. He used to leave them around the house and occasionally I used to help myself to one.

It is at this point that the long arm of coincidence appears. Barely 12 hours after I had typed this about Michael, my wife Judy, who had been reorganizing some books on a shelf upstairs, appeared with what had fallen out of one of them - a newspaper cutting of February 1994 that I had completely forgotten. It was Moira Shearer's critique in the Daily Telegraph of a biography of Michael Ayrton written by his step granddaughter, Justine Hopkins. It appears that my reservations about Michael were well founded. Apparently Joan was not his wife but a "charming woman, Joan Walsh." Michael "enjoyed roistering with the likes of Dylan Thomas and Constant Lambert. . . before running off with the wife of best selling novelist Nigel Balchin, Elisabeth". Balchin's best selling book was "The Small Back Room" later made into a film.

. . . . . . . . . . . . .

Dale was as good a place as any for a boy in the war. Lots going on yet a comparatively safe place to be, give or take the odd stray mine. Excitement had not left our lives entirely however, because in 1947 the country was gripped by one of the hardest winters in memory. Even Dale and Marloes, surrounded on three sides by the sea, did not miss out on heavy snowfalls followed by hard frosts. Both villages were cut off for weeks. At first this was great fun but as the Arctic winter persisted, it became a problem for me. There was no school for a good part of the Easter term and I was now in the first year of the 6th form taking Chemistry, Botany and Zoology for Higher School Certificate (all to be taken and passed simultaneously). I was also taking Physics, which I had dropped in the 4th form so as to continue with Latin, for a supplementary School Certificate and I had lost most of an important term.

Some food supplies from Milford had been landed on Dale beach after a couple of weeks but a week or two later, food was again short. A tractor and trailer was supplied by one of the farmers and a group of volunteers, no shortage of those, was coordinated by Gwyn James, the husband of Marjorie who kept the shop with her mother, Mrs Roch. We were well clothed for the ride on an open trailer in the freezing temperature. Equipped with shovels we set off for the journey to Haverfordwest which took over 3 hours. I don't remember that we had to dig ourselves out too much. Having obtained our supplies we got back in the late afternoon and the siege had been lifted.

. . . . . . . . . . . .

On the evening of 9th March 1948, my father was writing to Walter Bennett, formerly a Royal Marine sergeant at H.M.S. Goldcrest and a regular Sunday evening visitor to the School House. He had returned to civilian life as an accountant in Stoke on Trent and had become a good friend. My father had some good news to tell Walter. My mother's uncle, Owen Williams of St David's and a widower without children, had died some 8 weeks before and the Sime family with two other cousins were the 8 beneficiaries. After various bequests had been made the residue was to be divided equally among the eight nephews and nieces. As he had just written in his letter, my mother's share was a useful amount and quite enough to pay off his overdraft with a handy sum to spare. Life from now on was going to be much easier. Perhaps he was thinking that there were hopes of a small grand piano after all. I hope these were the thoughts in his mind as he suddenly lost consciousness. Dr Rice came out from Milford but nothing could be done and he died at home a couple of hours later of a cerebral haemorrhage. He was 48.

## POSTSCRIPT

After my father's death we moved to St David's where my mother was able to share her uncle's rented house with her single sister Chrissie. The Youngs, father John, his wife Meg and son Monty kept a close eye on us and were supportive in many ways. By this time John Young had to sell the farm because Monty was no longer fit to work on a dairy farm. He had developed severe eczema as a result of an allergy to cows and had also sustained a serious back injury. His sister Mary was at first heart broken at having to leave St Brides because, although she had many admirers, she was as involved in the farm as much as anybody. Fortunately her heartbreak was soon mended after meeting and in due course marrying the new owner, Donald Bagley.

On New Year's Eve 1948 the Youngs' invited me to a real Scots Hogmanay at Druidstone House, which is now the Druidstone Hotel, beautifully situated on the coast between Broad Haven and Newgale. For nearly 30 years it had been the Kensington family summer home after selling up the St Brides estate. The Kensingtons had lent it to Mr Young whilst he was building a house for his retirement in Haverfordwest. Mary and one or two other ladies wore kilts whilst all the men except me wore dinner jackets. It was quite a party.

I was taking a cigarette from my packet when a distinguished looking gentleman whom I hadn't met offered me one of his Woodbines but my tastes had become more refined for I liked Players. Here I dropped yet another brick. I declined his Woodbine and pressed on him a Player. Being a gentleman he put his Woodbines away and gracefully accepted one of my Players. He was more used to meeting Lords and Ladies, even Princes and Prime Ministers rather than gauche, maladroit teenagers like me. I was greatly embarrassed later when he was pointed out to me as Captain John Treasure Jones, Captain of the Cunard Liner, the Queen Elizabeth. He was a Pembrokeshire man who found it refreshing to return to his native county from time to time, a wise man indeed.